LEADERSHIP IN THE
AGE OF NOT KNOWING

LEADERSHIP IN THE AGE OF NOT KNOWING

Strategies for
Leading in a Learning Way

Mary Ann Rainey and Jonno Hanafin

First published in 2023 by NTL Institute

NTL Institute is an imprint of Libri Publishing

Copyright © Mary Ann Rainey and Jonno Hanafin

The right of Mary Ann Rainey and Jonno Hanafin to be identified as the authors of this work, has been asserted in accordance with the Copyright, Designs and Patents Act, 1988.

The authors are members or affiliates of NTL Institute for Applied Behavioral Science. Views expressed are those of the authors alone.

ISBN Paperback: 978-1-911450-64-1
ISBN Hardback: 978-1-911451-12-9

All rights reserved. No part of this publication may be reproduced, stored in any retrieval system or transmitted in any form or by any means, electronic, mechanical, photocopying, recording or otherwise, without the prior written permission of the copyright holder for which application should be addressed in the first instance to the publishers. No liability shall be attached to the author, the copyright holder or the publishers for loss or damage of any nature suffered as a result of reliance on the reproduction of any of the contents of this publication or any errors or omissions in its contents.

A CIP catalogue record for this book is available from The British Library

Design by Carnegie Book Production

Libri Publishing
Brunel House
Volunteer Way
Faringdon
Oxfordshire
SN7 7YR

Tel: +44 (0)845 873 3837

www.libripublishing.co.uk

To my mom, Lila Jenkins Rainey; my dad, Rev. Bennie Rainey Sr.; my brothers: James Rainey, Junior (Benny) Rainey, Reginald Rainey Sr. and Edward Rainey Sr.
Mary Ann

To the memory of Dr. Herbert A. Shepard
(17 September 1919 – 2 August 1985)
My teacher, mentor, colleague and friend, who ignited my learning and inspired me to lead
Jonno

We jointly dedicate this book out of love for our dear friend and teacher Dr. John Dale Carter, whose time and commitment to our personal and professional growth and development know no equal.

ACKNOWLEDGEMENTS

Mary Ann Rainey

My gratitude goes to my husband, Elias Tolbert Sr. It was Elias who brought the heating pad when my back was knotted in cramps from sitting for long periods of time at the computer, who gave me shoulder massages when they curled to my keyboard, who prepared meals to the finest details of my liking and who tolerated my bursts of senselessness when I lost my way. He would simply 'be there' until I found myself again. And like their father, our sons, Elias Jr. and Jason, gave me the same kind support from afar.

I acknowledge my mom, Lila Jenkins Rainey, who was my lived experience of a servant leader and my dad, Rev. Bennie Rainey Sr., who spent time telling me and the world that I was a genius. Who would suffer a lack of confidence in a household with this kind of love? Well, my four brothers – James, Junior (Benny), Reggie and Edward. I was the only girl and a middle child, and honed my power of influence on them. In spite of the havoc that I sometimes created, they were always my first followers.

Miss 'Chick' Wade, my kindergarten teacher, provided some of my early leadership experience, beginning at three years old. She would leave me in charge when she stepped away from the class.

Jonno Hanafin has been my dear friend and partner for more than 30 years. What I cherish about Jonno is his tender-hearted way of partnering; his loyalty; his wonderful, exquisitely timed humor; and that he feels, sees, hears and acknowledges me. Jonno never gave up on his dream of our writing a leadership book together, which kept me inspired.

ACKNOWLEDGEMENTS

Dave Kolb remains my teacher and mentor. As his student, he involved me in numerous projects that expanded my knowledge of Experiential Learning Theory. My thanks go to Richard Boyatzis, who together with Dave developed the Executive Skills Profile, a brilliant leadership assessment instrument which is the template for the leadership development tool that Jonno and I created for this book. And thanks also go to Alice Kolb, whose work with Dave keeps my learning about Experiential Learning Theory current.

Alison France shared the first article on our leadership model with Paul Jervis at Libri Publishing, who then invited us to write this book. Pat Arnold put us on the right path with her early feedback. Kate Cowie read every draft and provided meticulous editing. Kate and Yvette Hyater Adams were instrumental in securing the NTL Institute imprint.

My appreciation goes to my Gestalt teachers and role models: John D. Carter, Edwin Nevis, Elaine Kepner, Gwen 'Sharada' Wade, Claire Stratford, Frances Baldwin, Lynne Kweder and Carolyn J. Lukensmeyer; to John Nkum and Chantelle Wyley, who always expanded my thinking while working with Jonno and me in our international Gestalt programs; to the faculty of the international Gestalt programs; to my dear friend and colleague Brenda Jones, who never failed to ask how my writing was coming along, and to some of the leaders from whom I have learned: Mee-Yan Cheung-Judge, Bill Dunbar, Joachim Hasenmaier, Sheree Johnson-Gregory, Day Kornbluth, Donald Laackman, Jay Morris, Mark Newton, Anna Noonan, John Rowe and Deirdre Tejada.

A special thanks to Patrice Louvet for his generous and thoughtful foreword to this book. The staff at Libri Publishing have been beyond patient. Thank you for honoring my process.

ACKNOWLEDGEMENTS

Jonno Hanafin

First, I acknowledge the two incredible women I am blessed to have at the core of my life: my wife, Julie, and my daughter, Bri. Julie teaches me about commitment by living it every day. Her tireless and selfless support for my traveling around the world, doing what I love, comes in reminding me that she knew what she was getting into. I thought I knew what love is until Bri came into my life. Her gentle courage and consistent rising to the occasion inspire me daily. The love and kindness I absorb from my ladies replenishes the best in me when I am weary. Thank you, my loves.

My fellow-immigrant parents, Nancy and Phil Hanafin, taught me to move forward relentlessly in the face of unending obstacles.

Herb Shepard was a pioneer in the field of OD and a once-in-a-lifetime role model who saw what I was capable of long before I did. My fledgling confidence when taking on the massive Syncrude Canada startup at 25 years old was solely a product of his belief in me. He taught me to trust my instincts. That and he are still with me today.

My teachers and colleagues at the Gestalt Institute of Cleveland helped me become more integrated and more of me in all aspects of life. I am deeply grateful for the brilliance and humanity of John Carter, Edwin Nevis, Claire Stratford, Elaine Kepner, Gwen (Sharada) Wade, Lynne Kweder and Carolyn Lukensmeyer.

I am forever indebted to the wonderful women and men it has been my privilege to have worked with over 45 years as clients, managers, and partners. Whether they trusted me, guided me or occasionally took my advice, I have learned and benefited greatly from their counsel and friendship. I especially thank Michael Kitson, Brent Scott, John Brumsted, Denis Courtney, Jim Kochalka, Ismail Amla, John Nkum, Chantelle Wyley, Lisa Mascolo, Rad Wilson, Denni Gallagher, Michael Levy, Mitch Kosh, Bill Paul, Dorothy Siminovitch, Justin Jaschke, Hal Reiter, Sandy Helton, Chris Meyer, Ronald Slaats, Jim O'Hern, Wayland Hicks, Grant Howell, Cortney Cahill, Sean Collins, Al Gobeille, Theresa Cole, Roseann Lynch, Rick Day, John Howard, Cor Hoekstra, Bryan Zaslow, Sarah Engel, Nora Dunleavy, the Mod Squad, all the Rainmakers, Catalysts, IOSDers and my treasured colleagues at the iGOLD Center. A special thanks to Patrice Louvet for his generous and thoughtful foreword to this book.

And last but farthest from least, my writing and professional partner, Mary Ann Rainey. Our shared love of learning, Gestalt, teaching, leadership, difference, mathematics, challenging organizations and ultimately each other led us to partner often in our client work. We co-chair the International Gestalt Organization and Leadership Development (iGOLD) Program. For years, Mary Ann and I have talked about co-authoring a book on leadership and learning. As is often the case with practitioners, especially in my case, doing the work is my primary form of resistance to writing about it. With Mary Ann's help, I have finally marshaled the energy, and this book is the result. I could not and would not have done it without her.

FOREWORD

Patrice Louvet, President & CEO, Ralph Lauren

"When you stop learning, you start dying."

Albert Einstein

Mr. Einstein's statement may seem extreme on the surface, but its spirit is powerful, and its message is simple: learning delivers growth. And when the learning stops, so does growth.

Learning has always been a hallmark of leadership and, as Mary Ann Rainey and Jonno Hanafin convincingly illustrate, today's environment makes it a prerequisite. They contend we are in the "Age of Not Knowing" – a bad time, in other words, for a leader to think they have all the answers. Not only are there more dots for leaders to recognize, but more pressure to connect them. One thing we can say with confidence amid all the volatility and uncertainty: things aren't poised to become any simpler or slower.

Jonno and Mary Ann are excellent guides for such times. As behavioral scientists and leadership coaches, their advice is refreshingly concrete and clear. And it's backed up by a combined nearly 100 years of experience working directly with global leaders.

It's somehow fitting that Mary Ann and Jonno have, for years, worked with leaders at Ralph Lauren, a business I have the honor to serve as President & Chief Executive Officer. I say it's fitting because the company exemplifies the power of the principles they write about in these pages. Ralph Lauren started in 1967 with one man, who had no formal design training or business degree, selling distinctive ties out of a drawer in the Empire State Building. The journey from that single drawer to becoming one of the world's leading luxury lifestyle companies was fueled by Ralph's commitment to learning – learning how to bring his dream to life, how to stay true to his vision while also finding new ways to share it with the world – and how to build a team of talented people and guide them along the journey for close to 60 years now.

Before I had the chance to partner with – and learn from – Ralph himself, my own career had taught me how closely interwoven leadership was with learning. A formative moment came when I was asked to lead a business line for Procter & Gamble out of Kobe, Japan. The business was underperforming, and I came in and felt the need to move quickly – too quickly, as it turned out. Six months in, a member of my executive team had the courage to speak up and tell me some of the team felt confused by the direction. I had two choices in that moment, really: ignore the feedback and keep charging forward, or listen and see what I could learn. In the moment I felt pressure to drive progress and change, especially as a newly promoted General Manager. The second choice (which, as you can hopefully guess, was the one I made) wasn't comfortable given the time and business pressure I was under, but it was ultimately better for my team, for the company, and for my own growth and performance as a leader. That feedback helped us chart a new course – together. And it taught me a lesson I still carry to this day: there is wisdom in "going slow to go fast."

Stories like mine are peppered throughout *Leadership in the Age of Not Knowing: Strategies for Leading in a Learning Way* (stories like Ralph's are a little harder to come by). Alongside those stories of leadership are practical frameworks to implement their lessons – clarifying the actual behaviors and changes that position you to "lead in a learning way." They compellingly make the case that this style of leadership is, at its core, about being more effective. Which kind of leader would you bet on succeeding or want to work with: the one who spends more time listening and learning, or the one who spends more time talking and telling? The one who guides, or the one who dictates?

As Jonno and Mary Ann also remind us, leading in a learning way is not a one-time decision but rather an ongoing commitment.

It's a spirit that Ralph, in one of my favorite lines of his, has spoken to: "I always feel like I have to keep going," he said. "You can sit back and say, 'Maybe I can stop.' But then you're yesterday, and I love tomorrow."

Patrice Louvet
March 2023, New York City

PREFACE

This book has been in the making for more than 20 years. We see that now in hindsight. It is not that for all this time we did not have a desire to author a book. Rather, when we began writing, we could see our paths and destiny more clearly.

We share an educational background in mathematics, which set the direction of our professional lives until we were both lured away by the people side of organizations – Jonno to organization development and Mary Ann to organizational behavior. And even though our early travels in leadership and learning found us in the same galaxy, we were circling in different orbits. That all changed when we touched down in Cleveland, Ohio in the late 1980s and joined a premier group of educators and learners at Case Western Reserve University (Case) and the Gestalt Institute of Cleveland (GIC). In addition to their proximity to each other, the two institutions had a special connection. Five graduates of Case's doctoral programs founded GIC's renowned Organization & Systems Development (OSD) Program.[1] Our participation in the OSD program facilitated our meeting each other and marked the beginning of our enduring friendship and partnership.

---

1 In 1977, Edwin C. Nevis, Elaine Kepner, Leonard Hirsch, Carolyn Lukensmeyer and John D. Carter founded the Organization & Systems Development Program at the Gestalt Institute of Cleveland.

Our mentors had a special connection as well. Jonno apprenticed with Herb Shepard, a pioneer in theory and practice in organization development and leadership. Herb founded the Department of Organizational Behavior at Case and was a constant source of guidance for Jonno. Mary Ann was a teaching assistant to Dave Kolb at Case as he led research in learning theory and organizational behavior. It was during this time that Dave was also chairperson of the Department of Organizational Behavior. Dave and management and leadership theorist Richard Boyatzis developed an instrument for assessing executive skills based on Experiential Learning Theory that Mary Ann used in her research for her doctoral dissertation. This is also when she became intrigued by the adaptive qualities that learning and leadership have in common. Working alongside Herb and Dave, together with our experience as leaders, as executive coaches and as teachers, informed and incited our passion for on-going study of learning and leadership.

Our Objective

We describe the current era in which we find ourselves as the 'Age of Not Knowing' (or 'ANK'), where no one really *knows* what is coming next nor how to respond most effectively. Today's leaders are not only changing the tire while they drive, they are learning how to change a type of tire they have never seen before. Original leadership models were based on, one, learning how to lead, and two, executing what was taught. But leadership is not a dance of two-step. Our model is based on current reality, which requires leaders to dance to the tempo of the unexpected. Who is ready for the disruption of a game-changing breakthrough technology that can render their business model obsolete overnight? Where is the rule book for dealing with a pandemic that is impacting the company, its employees, and the professional and personal lives of everyone on the planet? What does a leader do when the murder of a Black man captures worldwide sentiment and demands an immediate response from their company despite diversity, equality and inclusion having not been 'real' priorities? The Age of Not Knowing puts a premium on learning, learning collaboratively, learning quickly and learning effectively.

Fundamental to our thinking is that leadership intelligence and institutional intelligence ought to be at least as compelling as artificial intelligence. The attractiveness of artificial intelligence is that it learns from experience. So do good leaders. During this time of unprecedented uncertainty, ambiguity and chaos in our world, we feel assured in our belief that leaders have no other choice except to focus on learning. As self-confessed learning junkies, encouraging leaders to operate from a mindset of continuous learning is our goal. Successful leaders are ones who have a healthy – in some cases, insatiable – appetite for learning. And like the two of us, who find teaching one of the ways to force-feed our learning appetite, forward-thinking leaders teach their followers how to learn too. This is the enduring impact of good leadership – leaving a legacy of people and organizations that are invested in continuous learning.

Our Writing Journey

Finishing this book was painstakingly slow. We were reminded over and over again that continuous learning can be brutal. Our endless absorption of new information, thoughts and insights forced us to rethink, reframe and rewrite constantly. Thanks to the gods for technology. Writing online brought some kindness to the never-ending process of 'adaptive writing'. Adaptation for us was like stepping into a stream, in the sense that the minute we stepped in, the water had flowed onward. Much like the process of change, our edits were non-stop. A hard lesson was understanding that once in a while we needed to stand still and allow the water to wash over, through and around us. Surprisingly, during those moments, nuggets of insight were left behind for us to gather. One of the biggest learnings was to go with the flow. And in almost contradictory fashion, we recognized that at some point we needed to step out of the stream and accept what we had. Of course, our publisher is pleased that we finally stepped away. Our learning styles are different, as are our teaching and writing styles: Jonno is more spontaneous, while Mary Ann is more measured. Fortunately, what served us well is our need to capture our ideas in ways that you, as a reader, find relevant, humanistic, smile worthy and maybe even quirky.

How to Read this Book

The seriousness of the topic of leadership moved us to dig deeply into both theory and practice. We wanted, at least, to keep the two balanced, whilst giving ourselves permission to lean more toward practice to make an 'easy read' of the seven chapters. Might we suggest that you first read the Introduction and Chapter One? The Introduction outlines the central theme of leadership and learning, and provides an overview of our stance on 'leading in a learning way' and the model that supports that stance. We hope you are intrigued by the idea of the *what* and the *how* of leadership that is presented. Showcasing the *how* is our way of making a statement about the true nature of leadership: it is about people! Chapter One has four sections that focus on understanding the foundations of leading and learning. Chapter Two through Chapter Six make up the core of the book, and are where we examine each component of our model more thoroughly. Even though these core chapters work together, each can be read as a stand-alone chapter. Each of them ends with ideas for practice. In the final chapter, we discuss next steps for us, make suggestions about the next steps for leadership and learning, and invite you to think about what is on the horizon for you on the topic.

Like our writing journey, we encourage you to engage with this book in the spirit of water flowing in a stream, letting the content and messages wash over, through and around you. We suspect that you will be surprised by the nuggets you find. Certainly, we hope you are stirred by something we say. Most importantly, we trust that you receive confirmation of some of the assumptions and thoughts that you hold about leadership practice. After all, learning does not mean divorcing oneself from what one knows. It means being open to exploring what is known and curious in the face of new and opposing ideas or ways of being.

We are grateful to have you with us.

CONTENTS

DEDICATIONS	v
ACKNOWLEDGEMENTS	vii
FOREWORD	xi
PREFACE	xv
CONTENTS	xxi
FIGURES AND TABLES	xxiii
INTRODUCTION	1
I. LEADERSHIP IN THE AGE OF NOT KNOWING	15
Chapter One	
Section A: Understanding Context	17
Section B: Understanding Change	26
Section C: Understanding Leadership	40
Section D: Understanding Leadership and Learning	55
II. STRATEGIES FOR LEADING IN A LEARNING WAY	65
Chapter Two: Relationship Mastery	69
Chapter Three: Vision Mastery	95
Chapter Four: Strategy Mastery	117
Chapter Five: Performance Mastery	139
Chapter Six: Presence Mastery	165
III. ONWARD	189
Chapter Seven: Learning for the Future of Leadership	191
BIBLIOGRAPHY	201
APPENDIX A: Summary of the RSVP Model	213

APPENDIX B: The Skills of *What* Leaders Do   218

APPENDIX C: The Skills of *How* Leaders Do Their Work   222

INDEX   227

FIGURES AND TABLES

Introduction

Figure A. The Experiential Learning Cycle   4

Figure B. The RSVP Model   9

Chapter One, Section B: Understanding Change

Figure C. The Learning/Acceptance Ratio in Response to Change   29

Figure D. How Organizations Function as Systems   37

Chapter One, Section D: Understanding Leadership and Learning

Figure E. Neuroscience and Experiential Learning   59

Figure F. The Gestalt Cycle of Experience   63

Table 1. The Clock Positions of *What* Leaders Do   67

Chapter Two: Relationship Mastery

Figure G. Key Factors of Relating to Self   75

Table 2. Tips for Good Listening   84

Table 3. Relationship Mastery   87

Table 4. The Relationship Mastery Usage Indicator   93

FIGURES AND TABLES

Chapter Three: Vision Mastery

Figure H. Providing Direction with Purpose, Vision and Mission — 100

Figure I. Reflection: A Way to See Ourselves — 104

Table 5. Vision Mastery — 108

Table 6. The Vision Mastery Usage Indicator — 114

Chapter Four: Strategy Mastery

Figure J. Strategy Mastery: Linking People, Purpose and Priorities to Outcome — 126

Table 7. Strategy Mastery — 130

Table 8. The Strategy Mastery Usage Indicator — 136

Chapter Five: Performance Mastery

Figure K. The Three Levels of Performance — 142

Figure L. The Ten Mindsets of Performance Mastery — 143

Table 9. Performance Mastery — 156

Table 10. The Performance Mastery Usage Indicator — 162

Chapter Six: Presence Mastery

Table 11. The Principles of Presence — 170

Table 12. The Choice Awareness Matrix — 173

Figure M. The Elephant in the Room — 178

Figure N. The Perceived Weirdness Index (PWI) — 179

Figure O. The *What* and *How* of Leading in a Learning Way — 182

INTRODUCTION

We all know the refrain, for it has been repeated countless times like the chorus of a popular folksong: life in organizations today is a story of unprecedented change. For those in the workplace, the typical day begins with more challenges than the day before. And change does not play favorites. No company is exempt from the magnitude of its disruption. Its impact is felt wherever people come together to pursue a common purpose – from the corner store in the rural countryside to the multi-national corporation in the urban center; from the government to the non-governmental organization; from the well-established small business to the start-up in a garage or at the kitchen table or on a street corner. Regardless of political persuasion, or religious viewpoint or work location, change will make itself known.

As organizations strive to cope with this incessant turbulence, sound leadership has become a critical undertaking. Because organizational effectiveness reflects leadership effectiveness, leaders are most assuredly feeling the pressure. If they are expected to step confidently into what is clearly a transformational role, both leaders and organizations are obliged to update their assumptions about what leadership is and how it is carried forth, and to create strategies to enable leaders to answer the call. The leader of the twenty-first century must possess skills to create a company culture that adapts, flexes, stretches, bends and sprints in the face of emerging dynamics. To keep pace, those showing the way must act with urgency on multiple fronts. Efforts must demonstrate the equal value of profits, people and the environment. This kind of leadership requires new ways of thinking and working if organizations are to continue flourishing.

Leadership in the Age of Not Knowing

This book is about *leadership*. It is also about *learning* and the value that learning brings to the practice of leadership. Our goal is to strengthen leadership success by providing ideas that are well-suited for the current reality of organizational life. Given the enormity of change facing companies, it comes as no surprise that know-how is in short supply. In a 2019 article, Mary Ann Rainey wrote:

> I think of the 21st century as the 'age of not knowing', when everyday experiences are so new and unfamiliar that we cannot easily discern what to do or how to do it. People expect and respond effectively to small bursts of change. Now they are bombarded by unrelenting disruption and volatility.[2]

During times of unprecedented change, learning becomes the best option for leadership. When defined holistically as the basic means by which humans adapt to the world, learning includes leadership. Both learning and leading are adaptive processes. Leaders who commit to learning inspire and motivate employees. Their organizations, in turn, thrive as the full range of talent and perspectives are utilized in new and exciting ways.

But leaders are more attuned to leading than they are to learning. We are inviting them to embrace learning as a distinguishing characteristic of how they work. Leading in a learning way involves convening diverse individuals with diverse perspectives to create, share, apply and retain knowledge at the individual, group and

---

2 See "Four roles of the Gestalt intervener: Holistic presence using experiential learning theory" by Rainey in Rainey and Jones, Brenda B., *Gestalt Practice: Living and working in pursuit of wHolism*, 2019, p.59.

organizational levels, and in the broader domain of the external environment, for the purpose of achieving organizational success.

The Foundations of this Book

Experiential Learning Theory (ELT), Gestalt theory and practice, and leadership theory and practice are the foundations of this book. The process orientation of ELT and Gestalt are well-suited for the adaptive requirements of learning leadership.

Experiential Learning Theory

Developed by David A. Kolb, Experiential Learning Theory[3] depicts learning as a cycle or spiral that results from the dynamic interplay among four primary modes or ways of learning:

- Concrete Experience (grasping)
- Reflective Observation (transforming)
- Abstract Conceptualization (grasping)
- Active Experimentation (transforming).

True learning requires 'touching all four learning bases', alternating between *grasping* (taking in) and transforming. An individual's immediate *concrete experience* of sensations and feelings is the basis for *reflective observation* of patterns and themes that are assimilated into concepts and theories through *abstract conceptualization*, which in turn constitute guides for *active experimentation*, application and practice. In ELT, there is no preferred way to learn, no learning hierarchy. Learners bring themselves fully to the learning process – sensing self, perceiving self, thinking self and doing self. Learning thus becomes a more holistic and integrative process.

---

3 See *Experiential Learning: Experience as the Source of Learning and Development* for some of David Kolb's early thinking on experiential learning (Kolb, 2015; originally published in 1984).

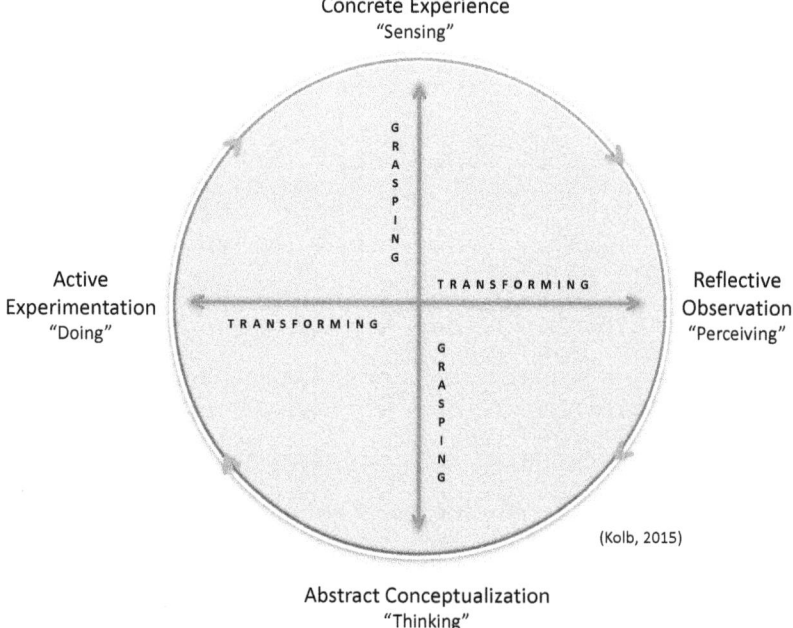

Figure A. The Experiential Learning Cycle

The Experiential Learning Cycle (Figure A) depicts the process of learning from experience.

Gestalt Theory and Practice

Gestalt theory and practice (Gestalt) grew from a theory of learning primarily credited to philosopher Graf Christian von Ehrenfels in the early 1900s. Von Ehrenfels coined the term 'Gestalt', a German word loosely translated as *form, configuration* or *whole*. He believed that a concept itself is different from the individual elements that make up that concept. Von Ehrenfels taught his music students that a melody is a fusion of notes and not simply a sum of notes. His ideas led to research by Gestalt psychologists at Berlin University who were studying perception. They postulated that the human brain helps us complete that which is incomplete. Also at the university during this period was social psychologist Kurt Lewin, who was conducting experiments on the impact of completing tasks and the release of psychological tension. In one famous study, his protégé Bluma Zeigarnick found that people remembered unfinished or interrupted tasks much better than they remembered completed tasks, a phenomenon known as the 'Zeigarnick Effect'. Psychologists Fritz Perls and Laura Perls, at the school as well, applied the concept of holism[4] to their emerging Gestalt therapy. Many of the perspectives on the practice of Gestalt in organizations today are taken from the Gestalt Institute of Cleveland's Organization & Systems Development Program. We are putting forth Gestalt primarily as a *stance* – a way of living and being in the world.

Leadership Theory and Practice

Our leadership model grew from integrating Experiential Learning Theory and Gestalt theory and practice with knowledge, models and tools from globally renowned scholars and practitioners of leadership and organization development, and our personal experience as leaders and working with leaders.[5] We were further informed by findings from interviews with 40 of today's leaders where we sought to get a sense of their experience in their job. They were asked to identify (1) sources of joy, (2) sources of pain, and (3) the key functions of their role as a leader. The summary of findings can be found in Chapter One, Section C of this book.

---

4 South African statesman Jans Smuts coined the term 'holism' in his 1926 book *Holism and Evolution* that is linked with his aspiration to create a league of nations. Smuts speaks of the existence of wholes and the tendency towards wholes and wholeness in nature. Fritz Perls first embraced Smuts' thinking on holism during the time that he lived in South Africa.
5 Thought leaders who influenced our writing include Sun Tzu, Harriet Tubman, Sigmund Freud, Wilfred Bion, Frederick Taylor, Mary Parker Follett, Kurt Lewin, Peter Senge, Abraham Zaleznik, Tom Peters and Robert Waterman, Martin Luther King Jr., Nelson Mandela, Ronald A. Heifetz, Marty Linsky and Alexander Grashow, and Brené Brown.

The Two Dimensions of this Book

We began this writing with the expressed objective of expanding on the Relationship Strategy Vision Performance Fundamentals of Leadership (RSVP) Model as presented in a 2016 article by Rainey and Kolb. The original version of the model highlighted *what* leaders do in four areas of proficiency. With Gestalt, we are able to address not only *what* leaders do (the content of their work) but *how* they do their work (their engagement style). Consequently, the RSVP Model is now a two-dimensional framework consisting of five areas of mastery.

The First Dimension: The What of Leadership

The first dimension focuses on the four fundamentals of *what* leaders do.

- *Relationship Mastery* refers to the ability of leaders to forge relationships and collaborate with others across the stakeholder spectrum, internally and externally. In Relationship Mastery, the leader is colleague, business partner, networker, coach, team builder and convener of communities.[6] Relationship (R) Mastery aligns with the learning mode of Concrete Experience.

- *Strategy Mastery* stresses the necessity for leaders to organize and structure the work. In Strategy Mastery, the leader clarifies enterprise-wide priorities, allocates resources and defines processes for achieving those priorities. Strategy (S) Mastery aligns with the learning mode of Abstract Conceptualization.

- *Vision Mastery* involves the leader gaining perspective, seeing the biggest picture and appreciating multiple realities as future possibilities are imagined. In Vision Mastery, the leader creates shared values, purpose, mission and direction to curate a desired company culture that engenders followership. Vision (V) Mastery aligns with Reflective Observation.

---

6 Peter Block writes extensively about the power of convening communities.

- *Performance Mastery* speaks to the leader as an agent of change, risk-taker and disruptor of the status quo – igniting entrepreneurial spirit and guiding the achievement of strategic priorities. In Performance Mastery, the leader influences, delegates, motivates, and inspires action and innovation. Performance (P) Mastery aligns with the learning mode of Active Experimentation.

The term 'mastery' is used to suggest a higher and deepening level of skill and competence. Learning leadership requires touching all four arenas of what leaders do. Leaders *grasp* (organizations and their environment) through relationships, transform them through vision, *grasp* them through strategy and *transform* them through performance.

The Second Dimension: The How of Leadership

The second dimension of the RSVP Model consists of a fifth component – Presence Mastery – that represents *how* leaders do their work. Identifying *what* leaders do is an important step; yet it is not enough. Leaders benefit when equal weight is given to the way they carry out their jobs. Indeed, considering that leadership is such a social and communal role, including the *how* of leadership makes perfect sense. A question for us as we pondered expanding the RSVP Model was: "Just how do leaders enact the duties of their job?" Our unequivocal answer was: "With their presence." This fundamentally addresses the leader's impact on others as relationships are forged, visions are created, and strategic priorities are identified and achieved through exceptional performance. Presence Mastery includes two sub-categories:

The *Four Roles of Presence* guide leaders in their use-of-self while interacting with others.

- In *experiencing*, leaders are aware of their personal experience and aware of others and the environment.

- In *noticing*, leaders recognize patterns and themes, and view experience from multiple perspectives.

- In *meaning-making*, leaders use theories, concepts, generalizations and metaphors to understand experience.

- In *influencing*, leaders aim to make a difference by applying theories and strategies to future experience.

The *Four States of Be-ing of Presence* support leaders in bringing their humanity to work.

- When *be-ing in love*, leaders are fully present in the moment with an open and extended heart toward self and those being led.

- When *be-ing in wisdom*, leaders seek enlightenment and insight through personal reflection and by engaging multiple sources of input, past and present.

- When *be-ing in justice*, leaders are able to assimilate knowledge through the exercise of critical thinking and by applying principles of fairness in decision making.

- When *be-ing in courage*, leaders take risks and move ahead with confidence and resolve despite the uncertainties involved.

The Difference between Relationship Mastery and Presence Mastery

Interaction with others is common to Relationship Mastery and Presence Mastery, though the intent is different. As a component of *what* leaders do, Relationship Mastery describes the types of interactions that leaders forge – e.g., with individuals, teams, the wider organization, networks, and donors and investors. As the *how* dimension of leadership, Presence Mastery centers on the impact leaders have as they engage with the various configurations of people. Figure B is an image of the RSVP Model.

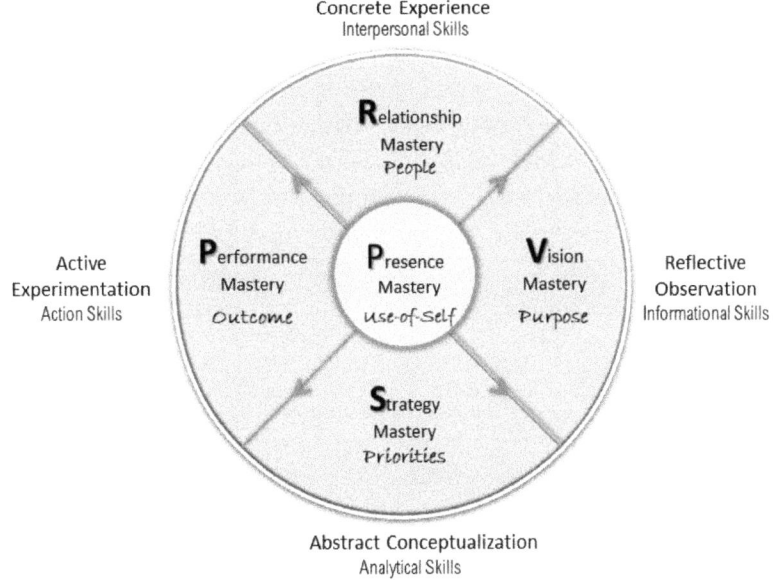

Figure B. The RSVP Model

About the Initialism: From RVSP to RSVP

The abbreviations R, S, V and P evolved over time. The story goes back to the Executive Skills Profile (ESP), a four-category skill assessment tool developed by Richard Boyatzis and David Kolb. The four categories of skills of the ESP correspond to the four learning modes: Interpersonal Skills for Concrete Experience, Information Skills for Reflective Observation, Analytical Skills for Abstract Conceptualization and Action Skills for Active Experimentation.[7] Rainey and Kolb recognized that the set of skills is connected to the key roles of leadership, as shown in Figure B.

---

[7] Details of the development of the Executive Skills Profile can be found in 'From learning styles to learning skills' (Boyatzis and Kolb, 1995).

INTRODUCTION

The abbreviations were first arranged as 'RVSP' to follow the cycle of learning but were rearranged to 'RSVP' to align with the *grasping* and *transforming* functions. R and S are *grasping* functions and share the north–south continuum of the learning cycle, and V and P are *transforming* functions and share the east–west continuum. Moreover, the abbreviation 'RSVP' has a familiar ring, given that it is also the abbreviation of the French phrase *répondez s'il vous plaît*, which means 'please reply'. Consequently, the RSVP Model is both a perspective on leadership and a request, asking leaders to say "YES!" to leading in a learning way.

Underlying Assumptions

1. The context of leadership today is characterized by novel change that is so unfamiliar that organizational know-how is in short supply.

2. Responsibility for meeting these challenges fall foremost to leadership.

3. Learning and leading are both adaptive processes, which makes continuous learning an effective option for today's leaders.

4. A theory-based, practice-tested, holistic and inclusive framework is required to lead in a learning way.

5. Leading in a learning way...

    a. is the intentional creation, sharing, application and retention of knowledge across multiple configurations of stakeholder, internal and external to the organization;

    b. requires the essentials of *what* leaders do: relating, visioning, strategizing and performing; and

    c. is a social process that involves *how* leaders interact with stakeholders, thus requiring leadership presence.

6. To lead in a learning way, one should...

   a. understand how learning happens;

   b. assess one's preferred way of learning;

   c. close the gap through development between the competence of the leader and the demands of the job;

   d. expand the range of the leader's presence;

   e. be intentional about learning; and

   f. apply the RSVP Fundamentals of Leadership Model.

The Contribution of This Book

Providing a *science-based* and *practice-tested* approach to leadership and learning is a major contribution of this book. Our stance is holistic, integrative, adaptive and rare in its focus on both *the what* and *the how* of leadership. Unlike behavioral, cognitive and other rationalist theories, with the RSVP Model, there is no declaration of one 'best' way to learn or lead. Neither is it our attempt to advance some 'great man theory'. Instead, we honor equal status to multiple ways of both learning and leading. We do not expect leaders to address all aspects of the RSVP Model with equal aplomb; yet they must understand that the essentials of leading must be addressed, if not by them, then by someone in their immediate circle.

Our Intended Audiences

This book is for leaders – and so, because everyone lives in an ecosystem where they are either leading or being led by self or others, it is for everyone. Nonetheless, we are directing our attention specifically to those who are in explicit roles of leadership, those who aspire to leadership, those who work with leaders – Human Resources professionals, consultants, coaches – and those interested in the study of leadership.

How this Book is Arranged

This book is divided into four main parts: introduction, opening chapter, core chapters and closing chapter. Following this introduction, the opening chapter will set the stage for leadership in the Age of Not Knowing with four sections: 'Understanding Context', 'Understanding Change', 'Understanding Leadership' and 'Understanding Leadership and Learning'. Strategies for leading in a learning way are found in the core chapters that consist of a chapter for each of the five mastery areas of the RSVP model. Included in the core chapters are the skills associated with the mastery area with detailed suggestions for practice. The closing chapter provides thoughts for future study and practice of learning leadership.

Summary

In the Age of Not Knowing, leaders must be prepared to respond in a world where challenges abound and solutions are in short supply – and have an even shorter shelf life. Continuous learning is an option to quicken the pace. In this introduction, we advanced the argument that the Relationship Strategy Vision Performance Fundamentals of Leadership (RSVP) Model provides sound theory and practical strategies for leading in a learning way. These are underpinned by Experiential Learning Theory and Gestalt theory and practice, integrated with insights from globally renowned scholars and practitioners of leadership and organization development. The RSVP Model attends to the essential work of leadership along two dimensions:

1. The first dimension consists of the four essentials of *what* leaders do (the content of their work): Relationship Mastery, Strategy Mastery, Vision Mastery and Performance Mastery;

2. The second dimension consists of a fifth essential – Presence Mastery – that represents *how* leaders do their work (their engagement style). Presence Mastery includes two sub-categories:

- The Four Roles of Presence (experiencing, noticing, meaning-making and influencing) that guide leaders in their use-of-self.

- The Four States of Be-ing of Presence (be-ing in love, be-ing in wisdom, be-ing in justice and be-ing in courage) that support leaders in bringing their humanity to work.

PART I

LEADERSHIP IN THE AGE OF NOT KNOWING

CHAPTER ONE: SECTION A

Understanding the Context of Leadership: What's Going On?

> Whoa, oh, mercy, mercy me
> Oh, things ain't what they used to be, no, no
> Where did all the blue skies go
> Poison is the wind that blows from the north and south and east.
> Marvin Gaye, 'Mercy Mercy Me (The Ecology)'[8]

> Mother, mother
> There's too many of you crying
> Brother, brother, brother
> There's far too many of you dying
> You know we've got to find a way
> To bring some lovin' here today, yeah…
>
> We don't need to escalate
> You see, war is not the answer
> For only love can conquer hate
> You know we've got to find a way
> To bring some lovin' here today
>
> Picket lines and picket signs
> Don't punish me with brutality
> Talk to me, so you can see
> Oh, what's going on
> Marvin Gaye, 'What's Going On'[9]

---

8 https://www.letssingit.com/marvin-gaye-lyrics-mercy-mercy-me-the-ecology-mm54lnz
9 https://www.letssingit.com/marvin-gaye-lyrics-what-s-going-on-pp13j13

CHAPTER ONE: SECTION A

We begin this first chapter with excerpts of song lyrics from the 1971 album *What's Going On* by Motown songwriter, singer and producer Marvin Gaye. The words are a great illustration of context, one of the first things we emphasize when working with leaders. Context is the set of circumstances that forms the backdrop of a company and informs leaders about what is happening in the world around them. With context, leaders see a bigger picture, which helps them decide what needs to be done. Failure to attend to context leaves companies vulnerable as they apply old strategies and processes to new realities. When we listen to Gaye's album, we feel the enormity of context. He covers so much – violence, war, crime, government, business, policing, climate, poverty, saving our children, power and spirituality. It is precisely this enormity that leaders must embrace, recognizing the multiplicity of forces impacting their organizations. Music aficionados refer to Gaye's opus as 'The Anthem of the Ages', while *Rolling Stone* magazine lists it as the most influential album of the twentieth century. Of course, the irony is that if we did not know otherwise, we would believe Gaye was writing and singing about our world today.

Context is a potent force because it is literally everywhere. This means that everyone and everything are affected. More than 30 years ago, organizational theorists Warren Bennis and Burt Nanus described the external environment as *volatile, uncertain, complex* and *ambiguous*. Still today, "We are living in a VUCA world" is familiar vernacular in organizations. The significance of context has a great deal to do with the scope of the leader's responsibility. Leaders are positioned at the boundary between their organization and the environment. Just to illustrate this interface, 'organization' can be an internal department, a division, a business unit or a larger enterprise, whereas 'environment' is everything outside the boundary of these domains. Keeping a finger on the pulse of both the organization and the environment is the leader's charge – forever looking in and out; near and far; up and down and all around to keep apprised of the current state of affairs. Then, they must adapt. Yet some leaders fail to see their job beyond their immediate territory, and not surprisingly, many of them who are aware of the territory remain overly involved internally. This is reasonable to some degree because inside the company is where most leaders spend much of their time. But it is not good leadership. Understanding context is a major component of leading in a learning way.

Trends and the Context of Leadership

Focusing on trends is part of understanding context. By tracking recurring business conditions and situations, leaders are better prepared to address impending threats and opportunities. Key questions for leaders to consider when examining trends include:

- Why are these trends important?
- What do they tell us about our industry?
- What are they revealing about our customers?
- What is the state of the economy?
- How is climate affecting our firm?
- What are the key social issues of our time?
- What are emerging markets telling us about the future?
- How do changes in demographics affect how we recruit, engage, develop and retain employees?
- What can we anticipate from the government and regulators?
- If we were our competitors, what would we be doing?
- What should we be doing to become prepared?

Answers could lead to switching from gas to electric, upgrading a technology system, or adding or discontinuing products and services in a segment of the market. Hence, the message to leaders is a*ssess what the future portends before you leap.* And though the external environment remains the bigger source of trends impacting organizations, the internal environment demands its share of attention. Increasingly, conversations about the context of change include internal forces, some of which are part of the list of trends we wish to highlight.

Technology

Technology is important because it comes with a distinct dose of perpetual change that is as complex, chaotic and confusing as change itself. Advantages and disadvantages are found. Obviously, technology brings easy access to data and information, and enhances many forms of communication. The arm of technology is long. Its reach is broad, extending beyond borders, companies and functions, and aids coordination and networking. Efficiency of processes allows more work to be done in less time. Another upside is that technology can drive down costs and democratize products and services, making them available to a broader segment of the population. One cannot imagine what the world would have been like without video-conferencing services in 2019 when life as we knew it suddenly disappeared at the outset of the COVID pandemic. Use of technology during the crisis resulted in substantive and, in many cases, permanent change in our personal lives and how business is conducted. On the other hand, technology comes with the high costs of hardware and software, the loss of jobs and the need for re-skilling, re-education and managing the impact on employee relationships. Globalization has been a beneficiary of technology, but it has brought with it concerns about security, privacy and access for all. A digital divide is evident across our world. No doubt, technological advances will continue, and those advances will be needed. The task for leadership is navigating the continuum of contributions and challenges that come with progress.

Globalization

Surprisingly to many, globalization has been around since the eighteenth century, but it ebbs and flows like the tide. The forces at play continue to impact business. Globalization is an economic concept that involves the interaction and integration of governments, businesses and people around the world for reasons such as safety, prosperity and peace. The initial attraction to these alliances was to tackle 'wicked problems'. These are cultural or social problems that are extremely difficult, or even impossible, to solve alone because of the magnitude of their complexity and other shifting variables. Examples of global partnerships are the United Nations, the World Health Organization, the Abraham Accord, Doctors Without Borders, the Association of Southeast Asian Nations and the African Union. In a sense, globalization is collaboration without borders. Unfortunately, nationalism, bilateralism, and quests for power and wealth have too many times created roadblocks to globalization. Fortunately, forward motion is propelled in some instances by agreements among non-governmental organizations and desire for peace after prolonged and devastating periods of conflict. The learning leader keeps apprised of the movement of the tide between multilateralism and nationalism because business and commerce get caught in the cross hairs, and consequences vary.

Customer Needs

Those guiding companies must anticipate the impact of change on the consumer. They must place the needs of customers front and center. Customer focus means value, quality, responsiveness, efficiency and reliability. In a 2021 survey, McKinsey & Company found that in nine of 13 major countries surveyed, at least two-thirds of consumers said they had tried new ways of shopping. Monitoring and anticipating customer sentiment are a leadership priority. On another front, companies are faced with social demands that expand their commitment to their patrons. Including ability, age, race, ethnicity, gender identity, sexual orientation and other demographic considerations in marketing and advertising is gaining more attention. Never has advertising been more colorful than it is today. Making technology cost efficient and accessible to disadvantaged parts of society has also proven to be of benefit to corporations. For sure, organizational social accountability is on the rise.

Climate Change

This trend brings urgency. Few companies, especially large enterprises, can ignore the impact of climate change. If they are part of the problem, many feel the pressure to be more environmentally conscious both in the products they offer and in their internal systems. When it comes to the environment, human health is of equal or greater significance than financial and economic concerns. According to research presented at COP26,[10] 80 percent of those displaced by climate change are girls and women. Customers are more likely to support companies that work toward a healthy ecosystem. Donors and investors, too, want to see how companies are limiting capital risks and minimizing disruptions in supply chains caused by climate change. Leaders must explore the part companies need to play in making the world sustainable. And this applies to small business owners who also can examine fuel consumption, use efficient appliances and participate in recycling efforts.

Immigration

In her 2018 *Harvard Business Review* article, Nataly Kelly[11] found that immigrants represent 27.5 percent of all entrepreneurs but only 13 percent of the US population. She goes on to show how immigrants are accustomed to change, are adaptable, risk-takers and entrepreneurial in mindset – all factors necessary for current business success. Furthermore, new entrants into the economy bring buying power for products and services. They expand communities. Their global experience is a built-in 'plus'. The contributions of immigrants to ethnic and linguistic diversity are immediate. It truly makes *poor business sense* not to include immigrants on employee rosters. Equally important, leaders must leverage the power of immigrants by creating welcoming and inclusive cultures.

---

10 Data presented by US Speaker of the House Nancy Pelosi in her address at COP26 (10 November 2021).
11 Kelly, 2018.

Diversity, Equity, Inclusion (DEI)

Like immigration, diversity has become a trend of global consequence to companies. With the help of technology and access to a range of social platforms, the world experienced shock waves in 2020 in the wake of such movements as Black Lives Matter, #MeToo and LGBTQIA+.[12] During the isolation brought on by COVID, these high-profile diversity issues found a virtual seat in board rooms and at leadership tables. They triggered personal and company soul-searching and forced a different kind of conversation about how disparity and bias are experienced and addressed in companies. More and more, we are recognizing that leadership is a mediating factor in diversity. With leadership comes power and privilege; yet leadership is rarely examined through the lens of diversity. Accepting diversity as a leadership responsibility spotlights the need for leaders to understand and respond to difference, equity and the fair treatment of those who are under-represented. It also heightens awareness of the links between DEI, power and authority, and social justice. The business case for diversity is solid. According to the US Census Current Population Survey, as of November 2020, job losses have disproportionately affected women; Black, Indigenous and people of color; younger workers; and workers with lower educational attainment or income. An opportunity exists for leaders worldwide to partner with public, private, non-governmental and not-for-profit

---

12 *Black Lives Matter (BLM)* is an international social movement formed in 2013 in the United States and rose to a global movement during the COVID pandemic as the world in its isolation witnessed the murder of George Floyd, a Black man. The mission of BLM is to fight racism and anti-Black police brutality. The group demands that society value the lives and humanity of Black people in the same way that the lives and humanity of white people are valued. *#MeToo* is an international social movement that raises awareness of sexual abuse and provides support to its victims. The term 'Me Too' was first used by US activist Tarana Burke in 2007. A decade later, the hashtag went viral as women came forward to accuse powerful men of harassment and misconduct. *LGBTQIA+* is an abbreviation for lesbian, gay, bisexual, transgender, queer/questioning, intersex, asexual and other terms used to identify sexual orientation or gender identity.

institutions to address barriers at work, for it is with diversity that learning thrives – and so does leadership.

Employee Engagement

More and more, employees feel detached from their organizations. The relationship between employer and employee no longer functions based on loyalty or long-term employment. Employees must be motivated in ways that are personally meaningful, for example, by offering flexible schedules, professional development that is consistent with career aspirations, working in teams and working from home. While working from home will likely shift from the high levels seen in 2020, it will remain a priority for some employees. Engagements also means human interaction where leaders take time to have conversations on a human-to-human basis with members of the company. The classic 'leading while walking around' is still effective.

Defining the Office

During the COVID pandemic, many companies were forced to allow employees to work from home. Surprise, surprise: productivity skyrocketed. With this proven success, the question is, what constitutes the modern workplace? The emerging thinking is that the office is wherever the work can get done effectively and efficiently. This perspective leans toward some combination of online and onsite work, but this idea carries concern. Many companies still hold expensive leases or own offices that extend to the clouds. Alternatively, the social capital accumulated by working in the presence of others is depleted during virtual interactions. An interesting fact is that, for many workers, working at home served as a 'filler of time' after all the binging on favorite movies and shows was finished. Now working from home is literally working all the time. Other challenges include personal responsibilities (e.g., child care and other obligations and distractions); the lack of spontaneous interactions; 'Zoom fatigue'; sitting for long periods of time, often incorrectly; and poor diet. How shall the physical and the digital operate? High on the list for leadership is the need to define the office… or maybe not.

Workforce Generational Mix

Older workers who, for a while, were staying on the job past retirement age are now opting to leave. The added need to work remotely using unfamiliar technology contributes to their decisions. Falling birthrates in emerging markets must be noted. Projections indicate low birthrates in parts of Asia in the coming decades. Declines in the number of workers aged 15–64 over the next quarter-century are forecast. Still, not all older workers are leaving. Some are staying as younger workers naturally join employment ranks. Conflicts arise from this generational mix, driven by differences in values, quality of life, approach to work, and attitudes toward hierarchy, patriarchy and commitment. Bridging the generational gap contributes to effective teams and productivity.

Summary

Leaders who ignore context do so at their own and their company's peril. Context is everything and is everywhere, primarily influenced by factors in the external environment but, increasingly, presented with challenges from the internal environment too. Understanding context informs leaders about the state of the world and how they might need to learn and adapt. Guidance can be gained from tracking trends that include technology; globalization; customer needs; climate change; immigration; diversity, equity and inclusion; employee engagement; defining the office; and workforce generational mix. Context is the breeding ground of change, which will be discussed in the next section.

CHAPTER ONE: SECTION B

Understanding Change: Run, Run, Run, but You Sure Can't Hide

In addition to understanding context, leaders must give forethought to the concept of change and their work. Any change in the environment means change for the company. 'Run, run, run, but you sure can't hide' suggests that there is no escape from the upheaval in the world around us. Like context, change is ever present, and today's brand is so unruly. It was Greek philosopher Heraclitus who stated in 500 BC that everything is constantly shifting and becoming something other than what it was before. Life is flux, he said, and there is nothing permanent except change. Centuries later, change theorist Kurt Lewin disputed the notion of a steady state in social systems, explaining that organizations are never stable. At best, according to Lewin, quasi-equilibrium is what is occurring. By accepting change as a normal part of organizational life, leaders can better prepare for some of its eventualities. Hanafin views change as the essence of life, and argues that leaders need only contend with the following three questions:

1. The purpose of change: Are the changes cultural, structural, administrative, operational, financial, etc.?

2. The ownership of change: Top, middle, bottom or enterprise wide? Leadership team, Human Resources, special project team, etc.?

3. The rate of change: What is the expected pace? Is it fast, moderate, or slow?

Managing Change?

The expression 'change management' is often mocked for the connotation that change can be contained. To those who are less cynical, 'change management' suggests the need to appreciate the complex nature of change and to develop informed strategies. It is from this standpoint that we have identified some core premises of change. Leaders can relate the premises to the laws of gravity and the strength of materials in design engineering. It is unthinkable to operate in opposition to them. A smarter option is to be informed and learn from them.

Premise A: Change is Driven by Personal Perception and Meaning-making

Change is conditioned, guided and controlled by our personal perception, and perception influences how we make meaning of change. This is a fact of change yet it is often ignored in practice. A common error for leaders is to make decisions based solely on their personal understanding and meaning-making, or on the inputs of a few individuals, usually from the top of the company. Broader involvement helps to understand the degree to which people are accepting or rejecting change.

Premise B: Personal Response to Change Varies

Too much change for some; not enough for others. People experience and respond to change differently. Some take change in their stride while others are overwhelmed and can only deal with change in small doses. In the midst of the COVID pandemic, Hanafin and Rainey[13] identified four responses to change:

---

13 The four responses were first presented in 2020 during the International Gestalt Organization and Leadership Development (iGOLD) Program, which shifted

1. ***Deny.*** There is no crisis here. This is not real. It is just another variation of what is normal or even a conspiracy. *Nothing* is required.

2. ***Endure.*** This too will pass. We will get through it, and soon things will return to the way they were. Let us *hold on and be resilient.* We will survive.

3. ***Adapt.*** Things are changing. A new normal is emerging. We must *stay aware of, modify and adjust* to what is emerging in order to keep pace.

4. ***Innovate.*** Let us reframe crisis as opportunity and seize the moment. It will have to be different, so why not make it better? We will *set the pace, create and shape the future* with compassion and confidence, and thrive.

Figure C depicts the *learning-to-acceptance* ratio in response to change. 'Deny' implies the lowest willingness to learn and the lowest acceptance of change. 'Endure' demonstrates some willingness to learn and accept change, though it is marginal. 'Adapt' represents strong openness to learning and acceptance of the need to change. 'Innovate' is the highest level of openness to learning and acceptance of change with the confidence to create new paths of products and services. When our clients are lost in the depths of change and cannot see the way forward, we attempt to help them cope by inviting them to identify where they are on the change continuum. We also leave them with this message: "Try your best to leverage the upsides of change. Become interested in what you are learning about yourself, others, and the company when it comes to change. You can look back but can never go back."

to virtual sessions because of the COVID pandemic. The decision to shift to online sessions highlighted the challenge of coping with unprecedented change for faculty and participants.

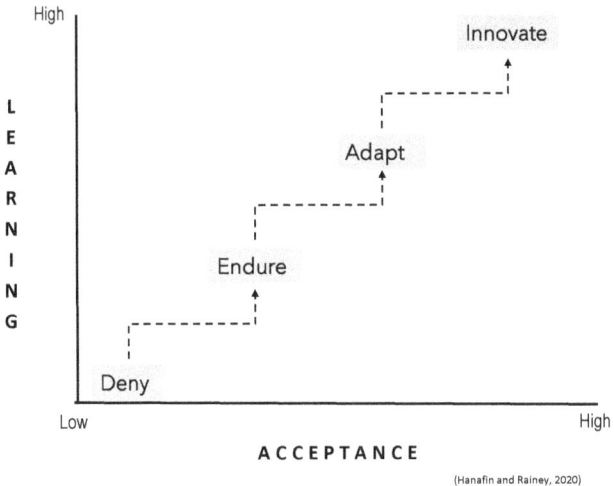

(Hanafin and Rainey, 2020)

Figure C. The Learning/Acceptance Ratio in Response to Change

Premise C: Resistance is the Manifestation of Multiple Realities

Most definitely, if you discuss change, you will discuss resistance to change. Yet resistance is seldom understood. In organizations, resistance is usually portrayed as a force of opposition from disgruntled employees or an outdated part of the business. In Gestalt practice, we learn to reframe resistance as the manifestation of multiple realities. Resistance is also a form of protection in the face of danger. As such, resistance becomes an indicator of health. At the most primary level, resistance can be defined as energy in another direction. It boils down to competing interests and commitments. Differences in the priorities of the sales and engineering departments is a classic case. The sales department is focused on the revenue generated by a quicker-to-market product, which is often at odds with the desires of the engineering department to have more time to design the best product. The push for speed from the sales department is experienced as resistant to the quality efforts of engineering. Yet, giving engineering more time undermines the sales group's priority to increase the bottom line. Leaders must perceive resistance as idiosyncratic and seen through the eye of the beholder.

Premise D: Change is Paradoxical

Change is paradoxical and not solely problematic. It manifests in benefits and burdens alike and can appear contradictory. Because change is so taxing, many find it difficult to consider any upside to the stress and strain that it causes. Everyone is affected during a rightsizing, those separated and those staying. Friends are gone, offices are rearranged, schedules and routines are altered, and, for some, a sense of purpose is lost. Grief is widespread. Ironically though, embedded within the dynamics of loss are seeds of growth and 'newness' – new relationships, partnerships and business opportunities. Think for a moment of the innovations that were born when the world sheltered in place. Virtual education, the delivery of healthcare and outdoor dining were all reimagined. Online commerce rises to astronomical levels during epidemics and pandemics. Leaders must accept that necessity is the child of change. A delicate balance must be stuck between loss and gain. We see this with innovations such as solar energy, electric cars and organic food offerings that grew out of restrictions placed on carbon emissions.

Premise E: Change has a Personality – The AFF Affect

All change efforts encounter difficulty in negotiating smoothly to their desired outcome. Three features accompany change: ambivalence, fragmentation and fluctuation. We refer to them collectively as the personality of change or the AFF Affect.

1. **Ambivalence.** For their own betterment, organizations must realize that change is necessary and evitable. Much of the challenge rests with the need that humans both seek and resist change, often at the same time. While most people in organizations would acknowledge the need for change, they resist moving from 'the way things are done around here', even when the things that are done around here are toxic.

2. **Fragmentation.** Consensus is rare during change. Typically, those at the top are not in sync with other parts of the

company. Unions are usually on different sides of change from management and leadership. Employees feel they know best about change, especially those on the front line. Even in the consultant–client relationship, agreement can be difficult to achieve. This fragmentation contributes to the challenges of creating momentum for change.

3. *Fluctuation.* Change is characterized by a series of starts and stops, ebbs and flows, detours and bypasses. Even the best-laid plans go awry. Consequently, the path to change is not a path at all, it is more an exercise in restarting, recycling and resisting. Sometimes, just muddling through is the best a company can do. This is when 'trusting the process' is useful.

Premise F: Three Perspectives on Change

We look at change in three ways: planned, unplanned and adaptive. Planned change is intentional. Unplanned change is emergent. Adaptive change can be both.

1. *Planned Change.* This is a purposeful effort of conscious design and action. A change strategy is in play. Examples include mergers and acquisitions, a new customer-service system, shifting to robotics, increasing diversity, changing hours of work and culture change. These initiatives include forethought, some form of assessment and analysis, and due diligence. In the field of organization development (OD), planned change projects are guided by Action Research – the classic, data-based methodology created by Kurt Lewin. Action Research is used in many fields but especially in OD, where it got its start. The phrase 'action research' should be taken literally: research for the express purpose of taking informed action. Several tenets are important in Action Research:

    - Practicality
    - Considering both human and organizational needs

- Partnering between members of the company and change practitioners
- A systems perspective
- Standing on democratic values.

Problem solving was the initial aim of Action Research. Today, planned change initiatives either concentrate on problem solving or build on what is going well using positive-change methodologies like Appreciative Inquiry. Different from problem solving, positive change focuses on inquiry into the strengths of a system and what is working well. Many companies prefer a balanced inquiry process that combines problem solving and reinforcing existing solutions. A reminder: planning change does not guarantee achieving change. Things can get highly disorganized, chaotic and disruptive, more than expected.

2. ***Emergent (Unplanned) Change.*** This unfolds in a spontaneous and unexpected way and requires a prompt response. There are two forms of emergent change. One involves major events such as when a top leader suddenly departs, significant public relations problems occur or there has been a quick loss of customers. Also think stock-market crashes and tsunamis. Companies have plans in place for some of these events, but it is when no plans are in place or the plans are insufficient that the situation is emergent. Furthermore, the timing of such occurrences is out of the control of organizations. What is needed from leadership is the ability to 'calm the waters'. Since most changes today are of an emergent nature, companies have now put processes in place where self-organizing, cross-functional teams come together to make fast decisions about emerging issues. Often referred to as 'agile teams', these groups use frameworks from software development and are particularly committed to working with their customers in mind. The other form of emergent change involves the day-to-day, moment-to-moment human dynamics that leaders

face. Here the leader is process consultant attending to group dynamics, facilitating a meeting that has steered off course, or adeptly mediating a heated conflict.

3. ***Adaptive Change***. Planned and unplanned change also fall under the heading of adaptive change. What is similar is the need to respond effectively to changing circumstances. Management and leadership consultants Ronald Heifetz and Donald Laurie believe the most important quality in leadership today is competence in adaptive change, which they define as the sort of change where organizations are forced to adjust to a radically altered environment:

Adaptive work is required when our deeply held beliefs are challenged, when the values that made us successful become less relevant, and when legitimate yet competing perspectives emerge. We see adaptive challenges every day at every level of the workplace – when companies restructure or reengineer, develop or implement strategy, or merge businesses. We see adaptive challenges when marketing has difficulty working with operations, when cross-functional teams don't work well or when senior executives complain, 'We don't seem to be able to execute effectively.' Adaptive problems are often systemic problems with no ready answers.[14]

What is needed with adaptive challenges is an extensive cultural reset and a change of assumptions, beliefs, thoughts and behavior across the enterprise.

Premise G: Four Types of Change

A commonality of change initiatives is moving from one condition to another. Differences in speed and impact are seen in the following four types of change we are underscoring: incremental, transitional, transformational and exponential change. Each has its benefits and limits but can be effective depending on the intent of change. What

14 Heifetz and Laurie, 2001, p. 29.

is problematic is when intent is unclear. By the way, introducing new technology as a change initiative fits into any of the four types of change. It depends on the scope of the technological change.

1. ***Incremental Change.*** Incremental change is the introduction of gradual, evolutionary, small steps built on the status quo. Such bite-size and easily digested chunks of modest change represent minor modifications to the current state and are introduced within the existing framework. There is minimal disturbance. For example, a new skill regimen that steadily increases in difficulty, a workplace continuous improvement initiative or a routine software update. The incremental approach assumes that development and change are the result of minor adjustments and alterations. Steps involved may be so subtle as to be unnoticeable. This is the case with the 'boiled frog' phenomenon. The water temperature increases so gradually that the frog is unaware of the change, and is therefore unable to remove itself from the life-threatening situation. But change is relative. Introducing agile methods in an organization accustomed to regular and rapid adaptation would be experienced as incremental change. However, in a more bureaucratic setting, agile could be perceived as transformational. Incremental thinking with any kind of change will produce, at best, incremental outcomes.

2. ***Transitional Change.*** (Not to be confused with transitional change as a phase or stage of change.) Change that replaces rather than builds on what exists is transitional change. Many auto makers are currently transitioning from fossil-fuel to electric vehicles. It is *moving from* to *moving to*. Transitional change creates discomfort and confusion, but its temporary nature mitigates significant disruption. The end state is known. This type of change often involves a transition period where the outgoing and incoming co-exist for a time. Having the old and the new occupying the same space for a while produces ambiguity but also comfort, similar to when the old and new computer systems run in parallel until confidence

is established. 'Grandfathering' is a strategy that often accompanies transitional change. A grandfather clause allows an exemption to persons or entities to continue activities or operations that were in existence before the implementation of new policies, rules, regulations and laws. Transition times can vary from one second, when, for example, a soccer team shifts from defense to offense, to, for instance, the 13-year transition by which Hong Kong was returned from British to Chinese rule.

3. *Transformational Change.* Transformational change is radical and requires people to examine and alter the basic assumptions about what drives and supports the current state. In physics, transformation is a conversion of one form of energy into another form. It requires the acceptance of discontinuity, that is, a sharp break with one way of doing things and the willingness to do things in substantially new and different ways. Crisis is often a support to transformational change, but not a requirement. It requires a change of social reality or a fresh perception and meaning-making. It also requires a shift in organizational culture (i.e., a change in the pattern of shared understandings). Once a company truly transforms, there is no going back.

4. *Exponential Change.* Exponential change is the most extreme and disruptive type of change. There is no option: adapt or die. Exponential change force-feeds acceleration into systems. The acceleration occurs at an increasingly rapid pace. In 2019, the world experienced the need to immediately shelter in place. This was the immediate end to a way of living as the world knew it. Exponential change can be seen as a compression of incremental and transformational change, with monumental increments and transformation on steroids. Instant adaptation and innovation are demanded with no existing playbook. Leadership models were not built for the extreme reality of 'all change, all the time'. Linear thinking is suddenly obsolete. Exponential change sparks an acceleration in the evolution

of leadership. New leadership models, like the RSVP Model, will be based on non-heroic leaders who include everyone to learn together fast. Learning is the only option in exponential change.

Premise H: A Systems Perspective is Still Useful

It was through the work of biologist Ludwig von Bertalanffy in the early part of the twentieth century that a 'general systems theory' (GST) emerged that linked both hard and soft sciences. Instead of reducing an entity to the sum of its parts, GST emphasizes a non-linear relationship between the parts and their connection to each other, the organization and its broader environment. Even with the limits of the GST principles of negative feedback and cause and effect, the *applicability of GST allows for* a more expansive picture of how organizations *function*, how they are *structured*, and at what level of system a leader might take action or *intervene* to influence change.

> ***Function.*** Input, throughput, output and feedback are part of how systems function. Organizational boundaries that are sufficiently open allow *inputs* from the external environment. Inputs include investments, donations, potential employees, suppliers, capital goods, technology, regulations, and industry and consumer data and information. These inputs are considered and used to improve products and services that are made possible by the integrated inner workings of a company, which are referred to as the *throughput*. *Outputs* are then returned to the external environment – as returns of investments or improved products and services. The level of satisfaction with the outputs is *feedback* and learning for the company, and influences the next cycle of inputs, throughputs and outputs (see Figure D).

UNDERSTANDING CHANGE

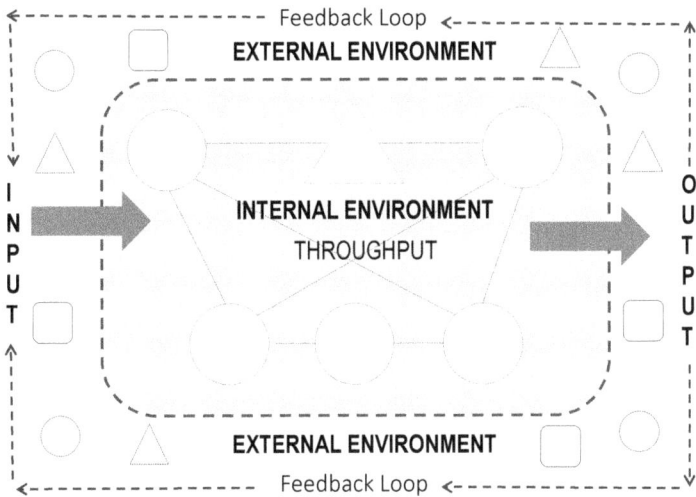

Figure D. How Organizations Function as Systems

Structure. Boundaries and borders depict how systems are structured. Obviously, one important boundary is the one between the internal and external environments. Both environments consist of smaller, bounded subsystems and networks that, in turn, are made up of subparts, and their subparts. This represents the embedded nature of systems. Internally, an organizational chart is one method for creating boundaries and internal structure. In an organizational chart, roles, responsibilities and relationships are drawn to convey a company as a whole or a specific department or unit. Hierarchy, another form of structure, becomes evident with an organizational chart. Structure is found in the division of labor. To illustrate, work can be conducted by individual contributors, two-party collaborators, teams at various levels, departments, divisions, functional and business units, and the total organization. Externally, structure consists of numerous subsystems that are defined by their purpose and character. Consumer groups, volunteers, organized labor, social activist groups, regulators, suppliers, bankers, institutions, and the broader community and nation are examples. Identifying, mapping and determining the degree of importance and the relationships (dependent, independent, co-dependent) among the subsystems signal the level of effort that needs to be expended during change.

Intervening. General systems theory tells us that what happens at one level of a system will affect other levels of the system. The impact will ripple throughout the organization. This dictates that intervening must be considered a very intentional and strategic act. And when we say 'intervening', we mean where will action be taken to influence what is happening in the organization? Leaders must determine the boundary or border that will mobilize the most energy and hold the greatest potential for achieving desired goals. Consider this: where would be the most promising place to begin an information technology (IT) initiative? The company's top leadership team? The IT leadership team? The CEO and the CIO as a pair? The CIO alone? The IT department? The whole company? Action taking has new meaning when leaders think systemically.

Summary

The subtitle of this section is 'Run, Run, Run, but You Sure Can't Hide', a popular expression that captures the omnipresence of change. One thing that can be said about change is that it is always nearby. It is also very complex, prompting various responses from leaders and employees, some of whom accept change more readily than others, who find it a daunting undertaking. Under the heading

'Managing Change?', we discussed several premises to help leaders better prepare for some of the consequences of change:

- Premise A: Change is driven by perception and meaning-making
- Premise B: Response to change varies
- Premise C: Resistance is the manifestation of multiple realities
- Premise D: Change is paradoxical
- Premise E: Change has a personality
- Premise F: Three perspectives on change
- Premise G: Four types of change
- Premise H: A systems perspective is still useful.

Understanding and accepting change as a routine part of organizational life is wise counsel for leaders. They also must understand the concept of leadership, which is the focus of the next section.

CHAPTER ONE: SECTION C

Understanding Leadership: We Love You – Then Again, We Don't

Because leadership is so complex, it leaves the world torn about what to make of it. This does not bode well for leaders. On the one hand, leaders are idolized. On the other hand, and just as passionately, the world holds deep-seated resentment for those who are in charge. We love our leaders – and then again, we don't. But despite headlines of excessive compensation, abuses of power and corruption, not all leaders should be imprisoned for life. Some are exceptional. Still, our experiences of good leadership are fleeting. If we reflect for a moment, it is easy to create a list of inspiring leaders from all corners of the globe. This same list includes leaders who left history with some of its darkest moments. Yet, our appetite for someone or some ones at the top never seems to satiate, which underscores the eerie dependence we have on leadership. And in times of crises, the reliance is more intense. In a 2014 article, Rainey and Kolb described this complicated relationship: "And even in our ambivalence, we have come to rely on leadership in all aspects of our lives – at home, at work, at play, in battle and where we pray."[15]

---

15 See Rainey and Kolb, 2014, p. 330.

The Evolution of Leadership Thought

The practice of leadership has been around since time immemorial. Early accounts are found in the ancient writings of Chinese general Sun Tzu's 500 AD *The Art of War* and in the treatises of Greek philosopher Aristotle. While not the first to come to mind when discussing leadership, psychoanalyst Sigmund Freud was a student, of sorts, of leadership. In his book *Group Psychology and the Analysis of the Ego* published in 1921, Freud explored the power of the group on members, but he also talked about leadership – though, not surprisingly, in very patriarchal ways. When examining the family unit, Freud referred to the dominant male, the father as leader, who controls the group and claims the female members. He concluded that the father figure is eventually killed by the strongest son, who then assumes leadership. Business consultant Mary Parker Follett figures prominently in the history of leadership yet is only now being recognized. This is for a couple of reasons: first, because she was a woman and, second, because her ideas were radical for their time, the early part of the twentieth century. Follett, also a social worker and student of Gestalt, encouraged organizations to rely on the person with the most knowledge of the situation rather than adhering to hierarchy and the advice of formal authority. Her work greatly influenced the practice of 'collective leadership' that is discussed later in this chapter.

Though leadership has deep roots, research and study of leadership are a relatively new domain. It was not until the second quarter of the twentieth century that leadership gained traction as a recognized field of study. Management thought appeared much sooner, growing from a need to formalize and teach the newer methods of production created during the Industrial Revolution.[16] For decades, management was the hallmark of business education in the Western world, as people moved into cities and factories were created to meet the demands of the growing urban population. Frederick Taylor's 1911 monograph, *Principles of Scientific Management*, set

16 See Wren, 1987.

the tone for manufacturing with its emphasis on 'one best way' of production. Efficiency and standards of output were key barometers of managerial performance. Later, beginning in 1923, the Hawthorne studies (discussed in depth in Chapter Two: Relationship Mastery) played a part in the recognition of people and relationships at work. Fortunately, as understanding grew about the complex nature of work, so did awareness of the value of attending to how people were led as well as attending to how they were managed. Once leadership grew as a profession, its ascendancy skyrocketed. A search of books on leadership in 2021 revealed that millions of books were published in that year alone. It is safe to say that leadership holds a grip on our global psyche.

A Noteworthy Leadership Study

Kurt Lewin and his colleagues conducted a seminal piece of research in 1939 that examined different approaches to leadership and the impact on followers. In the experiment, schoolchildren were assigned to one of three groups, each with a leader who led an arts-and-crafts project. Each leader created a particular climate – authoritarian, democratic or laissez-faire – then observed the children's behavior in the three settings. The findings included the following:

> ***Authoritarian.*** Lewin and his team learned that this approach to leadership, also known as *autocratic*, is strongly focused on both command by the leader and control of the followers. The authoritarian leader in the study saw productivity but it was unreliable. The members of this group stopped working when the leader left the room and conflict increased. Authoritarianism appeals to leaders who intend to make use of formal authority with little sharing of power and decision making, relying on personal instincts and thoughts. This form of leadership is best applied to situations where there is little time for group decision making or where the leader is the most

knowledgeable member of the group. Abuse of this method is usually perceived as controlling, oppressive and dictatorial.

Democratic. Children who completed their task in this climate were less productive than the members of the authoritarian group, but their contributions were of a higher quality. Moreover, the findings suggest that in a democratic climate, followers are more inspired, engaged and creative, which builds commitment to the goals. When the democratic leader left the room, the members continued to work. Leaders who consider the thoughts and opinions of others, work toward consensus but retain the right to make the final decision are usually attracted to this approach to leadership. Democratic leaders, also known as *participative* leaders, offer guidance to group members and may also participate in the group. Here, leaders must be mindful of becoming too deferential to the group.

Laissez-faire. Lewin noted that laissez-faire leadership tended to result in groups that lacked direction, made less progress and produced fewer outcomes. Conflict arose most often in this climate due to a lack of minimum direction. Members competed for positions, blamed each other and refused to hold themselves personally accountable. The laissez-faire leader sat back and delegated full decision-making power and authority to others. While this approach, also known as *delegative* leadership, can be useful in situations involving highly qualified experts, often it leads to poorly defined roles and a lack of motivation.

Additional Findings. The researchers revealed another useful insight: it is harder to move from an authoritarian climate to a democratic climate than vice versa.

They stated that authoritarianism is difficult to unlearn and that democracy must be continuously reinforced. Even today, we witness the impact of authoritarianism when we see the formerly oppressed becoming the oppressor. We conclude that organizational climate impacts worker attitude and behavior and the effects are long-lasting. Equally valuable from the Lewin study was the early confirmation of different ways to lead, each with its advantages and disadvantages. This study was a classic academic experiment yet very pragmatic – a characteristic of Lewin's work. Even after more than 80 years of scrutiny, it maintains its standing in the halls of prized research.

In 1946, Lewin and his colleagues convened a diverse group of about 30 leaders in New Britain, Connecticut, to study and train them in the most effective means of eliminating racial and religious prejudice. What was significant about the event was that Lewin, a German Jew who had fled Nazi Germany, had the courage to confront discrimination at this time in the United States. As he studied leadership, he modeled leadership. It was one of the first large group interventions on social change specifically designed for leaders. The conference was a precursor of the NTL Institute's Training Group (T-group) that focuses on self, interpersonal and group awareness and knowledge.

Other Perspectives on Leadership

There is no one generally accepted theory of leadership. As the context of leadership has shifted, so have expectations and conceptualizations of what it is. Leadership has been defined as an inborn trait found in certain people, as the characteristics shared by those who lead, as a social process driven by the interaction between leader and follower, by what leaders do, and by the situational and environmental conditions under which work is accomplished. Among the current forms of leadership that are frequently cited are transformational, agile, appreciative, generative, humble, leaders as stewards, self-leadership, and distributed leadership. What follows are summaries of perspectives on leadership that align with the core tenets of learning leadership. Each brings into focus specific dimensions that enhance the understanding of leadership. Similar variables can be found among them, although not necessarily expressed in the same way or with the same emphasis.

A. *Managing or Leading? Transacting or Transforming?* Much of the literature on leadership is devoted to comparisons between leadership and management. According to change theorist John Kotter, both management and leadership are necessary in large companies when the external environment is very dynamic. He further explains that as a company becomes larger and more complex in its internal workings, the need for management increases, and as the external environment becomes more dynamic and uncertain, leadership becomes more important.

In differentiating between management and leadership in 1978, James Burns compared ordinary (transactional) leaders, who exchange tangible rewards for the work and loyalty of followers, to extraordinary (transforming) leaders, who engage with followers, focus on higher-order intrinsic needs and raise consciousness about the significance of work. Transformational leadership is often regarded as the single most effective style of leadership. This approach to leading was first described during the late 1970s and later expanded upon by researcher Bernard M. Bass, who argued that transformational leaders motivate and inspire followers and guide positive changes in groups. Bass further maintained that transformational leaders tend to be emotionally available, energetic and passionate; not only committed to helping the organization achieve its goals, but also supporting employees to fulfill their potential.

B. *Shared (Collective) Leadership.* 'One-plus leadership' is a way to describe shared leadership because all expressions of leading are shared by a group of people. It refers to an approach in which, instead of emphasizing the search for and the development of leaders, attention is given to the creation of conditions in which leadership potential can emerge and flourish. Craig Pearce and Jay Conger state that an assumption of shared leadership is that everyone *can* and *should* lead. The authors trace the beginnings of shared leadership to business consultant Mary Parker Follett, who is known for encouraging leaders to embrace an attitude of power *with* others rather than power *over* others.

C. ***Servant Leadership.*** The phrase 'servant leadership' was coined by Robert K. Greenleaf in *The Servant as Leader*, an essay that he first published in 1970. He clarified the difference between the servant leader and the traditional leader:

> The servant-leader is servant first... It begins with the natural feeling that one wants to serve, to serve first. Then conscious choice brings one to aspire to lead. That person is sharply different from one who is leader first, perhaps because of the need to assuage an unusual power drive or to acquire material possessions... The difference manifests itself in the care taken by the servant – first to make sure that other people's highest priority needs are being served. A servant-leader focuses primarily on the growth and well-being of people and the communities to which they belong.[17]

D. ***Feminist Leadership.*** In her 2011 book, *Feminist Leadership for Social Change*, social activist Srilatha Batliwala reviews key definitions of Feminist Leadership and summarizes the common features:

a. They describe "a set of attributes/behaviors, values, and practices. They are often constituted by adjectives and verbs like inclusive, participatory, collaborative, nurturing,

---

[17] Greenleaf, 1970.

empowering, consensus building, valuing and respecting others, and valuing growth and development".

b. The definitions "deal with power and politics, dimensions that are almost invisible in the mainstream definitions of leadership, even of feminine leadership".

c. "Some of the definitions hint at the critical issue of feminists' own use and practice of power when they occupy leadership positions." (p.29)

Based on her analysis, Batliwala captures Feminist Leadership in a framework that is steered by the Self in four areas, which she refers to as the "Four Ps":

1. *Power*, because leadership at its core is about power in every form imaginable.

2. *Principles/values*, because leadership is affected by values that guide behavior and principles that guide actions.

3. *Politics/purpose* refers to the socio-economic conditions (politics) that are the backdrop for the company's mission and vision (purpose).

4. *Practices* that are concerned with the different types of work of leadership.

E. **Situational Leadership**. The influence of the environment and situation are stressed in situational leadership, developed by Paul Hersey and Ken Blanchard, and published in 1969 as *The Life Cycle Theory of Leadership*. This perspective describes four different leadership styles: *telling, selling, participating* and *delegating*. Blanchard amended the original four categories to better align the leader's approach to the development needs of team members:

a. *Directing* by giving orders and expecting obedience but offering little guidance and assistance

b. *Coaching* by giving lots of orders, but also lots of support

c. *Supporting* by offering plenty of help, but very little direction

d. *Delegating* by offering little direction or support.

The Dilemmas of Leadership

Management and leadership are similar in many ways, but one distinction comes in the form of the need for leaders to address the many competing priorities that come their way each day. We refer to these phenomena as 'dilemmas to be managed' rather than 'problems to be solved'. Problem solving is a key managerial requirement, while leadership is more in the business of managing dilemmas that have no clear-cut or black-and-white resolution. For leaders, it is not 'either/or', it is 'both/and… and sometimes even more'. Leaders are confronted almost exclusively with competing priorities and demands across the spectrum of their stakeholders. Consequently, we advise new entrants to the ranks of top leadership to develop the competence of living in the 'grey space' of dilemmas. We highlight several common dilemmas in leadership.

- *Process–People.* As push comes to shove, which it always does for leaders, do they go with the people or with the process? What is key is the ability to navigate the process–people continuum. Over time, processes become outdated and no longer serve the current need. When this happens, the leader is often called upon to adjudicate. The process is the means, not the end. It reveals how goals will be met efficiently. People determine whether the goals will be met effectively. The learning leader sets in motion the effort to redesign the process with what has been learned from and by people. Those who are knowledgeable of the process are in the best position to redesign it. It should be noted that processes guide but are not accountable. People are accountable, and leaders are accountable both for the process and to the people.

- *Action–Reflection.* To be or to do. That is the question. In the face of disruption, or just making things happen, leaders face the dilemma of moving with what they have or waiting for further insight to offer a better way. Overdoing either side of the action–reflection dilemma results in haste or inertia, both regrettable when unintentional. Action is supported by instinct, habit and a doing orientation. Reflection is encouraged by patience, consideration and perspective. The Holy Grail of decision making for leaders is informed choice. The fertile development ground for many leaders, particularly at the interpersonal level, is navigating the space between reaction and response. Reaction is automatic and unconscious. Reflection before action enhances the probability that the action will produce the intended effect by tempering the habitual autopilot response with situational consideration. Locating the suitable point on the action–reflection continuum allows the leader to sidestep impulsiveness and lethargy to deliver considered decisions.

- *Personal Relationship–Professional Relationship.* All relationships are dilemmas. The parties in the relationship must have their needs met to sustain the relationship in a manner that is balanced and mutually beneficial. The same is true with the personal and professional dimensions of the leader's relationships. "You have the job even though you are not the best candidate". "I have to let you go even though you are my friend". Like all dilemmas, an out-of-balance relationship is problematic. A relationship skewed too far on the professional side lacks humanity and soul and thereby limits the extent people can be their whole selves in relation to the leader and in the work. Over-reliance on the personal relationship creates a long list of professional boundaries to be managed. When a relationship is both professional and personal, the professional aspect drives the relationship. Leaders must consider each relationship based on how it effects other relationships and the perception of favoritism.

- *Performance–Learning.* Leaders are expected to walk and chew gum. Is it more important for a leader to deliver performance now or learn how to improve future performance? Yes and yes. Hence, a dilemma. The dichotomy is false. Current pressure of performance and getting rewards tempts leaders to forgo learning much like postponing equipment maintenance in the interest of continuous operation. Considering our belief that learning faster is the only sustainable competitive advantage; a useful reframing is from learning in hindsight to learning in the moment. This mindset shift requires explicitly declaring performing and learning as co-equal goals, where the leader is both chief operating officer and chief learning officer. When they inquire, they incite everyone to learn. When they tell, they confine everyone to performing.

The Current State of Leadership

When it comes to the specific work of leadership, global financial services provider Deloitte reports that 80 percent of the respondents to a 2019 survey believe that leading in the twenty-first century brings with it a unique set of requirements that are important or very important to their organization's success. Listed among the new requirements are *inclusion, fairness, social responsibility, understanding the role of automation* and *leading in a network.* More significantly, many companies are not satisfied with their leadership development programs. A mere 25 percent are effectively building digital leaders; only 30 percent are succeeding in developing leaders to meet evolving challenges. But companies first must have leaders who can be developed. With the impact of a global pandemic and growth in the gig economy breeding short-term contracts and entrepreneurship, the void of leadership is felt across all industries. Worldwide studies of senior executives and Human Resources professionals indicate that nearly three-quarters of North American employers experience a dearth of leaders. In Asia, the problem is even worse, according to management and leadership scholars Susan Ashford and D. Scott

DeRue, who found that 88 percent of organizations in the region indicated concern about a looming shortage of leadership talent.[18]

Our Interviews

As we mapped out the RSVP leadership model, we could not help but wonder what kind of experience leaders are having as they carry out their roles. We conducted a survey of 36 senior executives[19] through one-to-one interviews and written responses. The questions were simple: what aspects of the leadership role bring you joy? What aspects of the leadership role bring you pain?

A. *Sources of Joy in the Leadership Role*

Question: In your experience as someone who has been in a leadership role, has aspired to leadership or has had a follower role, can you choose five enjoyable aspects of your leadership experience? 'Enjoyable' in this context means that the experience was uplifting and satisfying.

The strongest theme among the leaders is power, in the sense of being able to make things happen. The ability to make a positive difference in the work and in people's lives includes fostering accomplishment and creation, cultivating camaraderie and growing human beings. The satisfaction of having plans come together in pursuit of a vision is made possible through their access to and deployment of resources. The leaders reported their personal reward comes in the form of feeling trusted to act and empowered to innovate. Recognition for their ability to get things done is not a motivator, but rather a welcomed by-product of their work. The participants in our survey asserted that alignment between the leaders' personal values

---

18 Ashford and DeRue, 2012
19 The 36 senior global executives were: 67% white, 33% BIPOC; 64% male, 36% female; 42% white males, 25% white females, 22% male BIPOC, 11% female BIPOC; and 42% CEOs, 11% COOs, 8% CHROs, 16% other C-level executives, 11% division presidents/directors, 6% board members, 6% members of parliament.

and those of the system they lead served to enhance their experience of joy.

B. *Sources of Pain in the Leadership Role.*

Question: In your experience as someone who has been in a leadership role, has aspired to leadership or has had a follower role, can you choose five painful aspects of your leadership experience? 'Painful' in this context means that the experience was unpleasant and distressing.

'It is business and it is personal' is a clear theme in this research. The personal cost of carrying out their role was identified by leaders as their primary source of pain. On the job, this took the form of letting good people go for lack of fit, experiencing betrayal and broken trust, and the sense of loneliness and isolation that came from having no true peer with whom to share and confide. Outside of work, the effort demanded in executing their responsibilities cost these leaders time away from their families, the burdens of frequent travel and being forced to miss out on significant life events. Most reported frustration with having their hands tied by bureaucracy or politics, and disappointment working with imperfect people who underperformed, let their egos get in the way and became lazy. Our leadership group struggled with the wasted capability brought about by the ineffectiveness of their organization's development process (including dysfunctional feedback mechanisms) that prohibited their correcting flaws and capturing untapped potential.

C. *Key Functions of a Leader's Role*

We added an additional question to the survey half-way through the data-collection process for a subset of the sample group (19 of the 36). This third question inquired about the key functions of a leader's role.

Question: What are the key functions of your job as a leader? Define 'key functions' as those aspects of your role as a leader that are so specifically fitted or suited for leadership that, without them, you would not be successful.

D. *Themes*

Four themes emerged related to the role of the leader from the responses. They are:

1. Growing, motivating, inspiring, empowering and coaching people, fostering collaboration and building powerful relationships

2. Guiding their organization toward a vision/mission; directing, organizing and looking ahead

3. Making hard decisions

4. Solving problems (hands on) and navigating to a goal.

After these four themes took shape on their own, we noticed they corresponded nicely to the four components of learning leadership of this book:

1. Growing people (Relationship)

2. Guiding in a direction (Vision)

3. Making decisions (Strategy)

4. Problem solving (Performance).

Our Definition of Leadership?

Studies suggest that the involvement of top leadership contributes most to the success of organizational transformations. In 1977, Abraham Zaleznik, professor of organizational psychodynamics at Harvard University, argued that when leadership is absent, it is more difficult for organizations to adapt to change, sustain super-ordinate goals and values, and instill a sense of pride of belonging among its members.

As the context of the world has shifted, so has the practice and experience of leadership. What constitutes good leadership in one setting is unappealing and even ineffective in others, making it difficult to find an agreed-upon definition. A growing point of departure is whether leaders should simply gather and guide followers or drive and direct them. The good news is that a convergence is taking shape. There is general agreement that leadership is a function of responding to the environment either through adaptation or by disrupting the normal order of things through innovation, all while sustaining the interest and support of followers.

The central theme of this book is 'leading in a learning way', which involves convening diverse individuals with diverse perspectives to create, share, apply and retain knowledge at the individual, group and organizational levels, and in the broader domain of the external environment, for the purpose of achieving organizational success.

Summary

Even though leadership as a school of thought is new when compared to management, leadership practice dates to ancient times. Leaders have brought joy as well as enormous pain, and this leaves some people torn about the value of leadership. Nevertheless, it is regarded as critical to the effective functioning of organizations. Because leadership means different things to different people, a single agreed-upon definition has been elusive. This likely accounts for the many theories, models and books on leadership. On a positive note, a few areas of agreement can be found: leadership is influenced by the broader environment, one's personal experiences and perceptions, and the needs of one's company and its culture. Leadership is subjective. Leaders are influenced and are influential, adapt and initiate, build and disrupt. Leadership is a social construct fueled by the relationship between the leader or leaders and their followers. Most of all, whether leadership is held by one or by many, it will fail without followership.

CHAPTER ONE: SECTION D

Understanding Leadership and Learning: Do You Mean I Can Continue to Learn?

Learning is a potent force of human existence. It contributes to human growth and development. Of particular significance to the study of leadership is the growing acceptance of the view of organizations as systems of learning where a leader's adaptive ability is a key driver of success. A 'learning organization' – a concept advanced by organizational theorist Peter Senge in the 1980s – facilitates the learning and transformation of its people and the company. Ron Heifetz and Donald Laurie, renowned authors on the topic of adaptive change, think the demands of our times require leadership that is committed to learning.[20] On the value of learning during times of change, social philosopher Eric Hoffer believes that continuous learning is the only choice:

> In a time of drastic change, it is the learners who inherit the future. The learned find themselves equipped to live in a world that no longer exists.[21]

---

20 Ron Heifetz and Donald Laurie outline the five strategic principles of adaptive leadership: diagnose the situation, keep the level of distress tolerable, engage issues that require the most attention while counteracting avoidance, give people responsibility that they can handle and protect those who speak out.
21 Hoffer, E. 1973, p. 26.

In a 2012 interview, former Israeli President and Nobel Laureate Shimon Peres predicted the increasing economic value of learning:

> The greatest branch of the economy in the future will be learning and teaching and educating. Learn more, work less. I think the proportion will change. Most of our time we will either be studying, teaching, or doing research. There is no end to learning, there is no end to research, there is no end to imagination – and no limit to creativity.[22]

Mark Thompson, former president and CEO of the *New York Times*, in a 2020 McKinsey & Company interview advised leaders to be open to learning:

> Many, many leaders have become leaders because they are great at one thing. Generally, in this digital moment, you need people who can be good at one thing and can then learn something else.[23]

Resistance to Learning

Yet learning is seldom prioritized by leaders. There are several reasons for this arms-length relationship with learning.

> ***The All-knowing Leader.*** One is the myth of the all-knowing leader, who does not need to learn anything else. Those at the higher ranks of leadership have bought into the hyperbole (hype) that once one occupies the top tier of leadership, one must not show gaps in knowledge. In fact, many leaders believe they have no gap in learning. Ironically, those leaders

---

22 Peres, 2012, p. 3.
23 Interviewed by Yael Taqqu, senior partner at McKinsey. https://www.mckinsey.com/industries/technology-media-and-telecommunications/our-insights/building-a-digital-new-york-times-ceo-mark-thompson

who value learning often resort to learning on their own terms, never admitting when they are learning. They literally steal the ideas of their colleagues, direct reports or others, and are what we call 'undercover learners'. Of course, this creates a distorted sense of self that is difficult to reverse. Moreover, accountability falls by the wayside. A learning agenda begins with the public support of the leader.

Learning Has an Expiration Date. Another factor is the belief that learning has a limited shelf life and stops once humans reach adulthood. This is not the case, according to Kathryn Papp, neuropsychologist at Harvard Medical School:

Until the mid-1990s, we thought that people were born with however many brain cells they would die with. We now know that the growth of new cells – a process called neurogenesis – occurs throughout life, even in older age.[24]

Research confirms that the human brain is pliable and capable of what is called neuronal plasticity. Furthermore, when the adult brain is challenged to learn something, like mapping a new work process or solving an unfamiliar problem, it changes. It is as if the brain's circuit board is activated, and lights go off. The adult brain can handle change – and will likely learn from it.

Learning Takes Time. Learning is easily sidelined, especially during complex change because it 'takes too much time'. Curiosity and inquiry do not have a chance. Consequently, the need to stay competitive and continuously learn are considered mutually exclusive. These stilted perspectives on learning put organizations on the fast track to failure. History has

---

24 Papp, 2015.

logged numerous stories of the toll taken when organizations are unwilling to learn. The case of the US automobile industry in the 1970s remains a timeless example of failure to learn. Unfortunately, leaders based their innovations on what was happening in the US. Their short-sightedness led to the collapse of an industry that took years to recover. Such a fixed attitude toward learning makes it difficult for leaders to look at anything familiar from a different viewpoint or, furthermore, to consider the unfamiliar.

Many Leaders Do not Know How to Learn. One of the main reasons for the lack of commitment to learning is simply that leaders do not know how learning takes place for themselves. Nor do they know how to bring learning to their organizations. They are perplexed by how learning happens and how to use it to help them make meaning of their experience. What they get is a good model but little guidance on how to apply the model on a day-to-day basis. Or they get a philosophy with no model or tools. Or they get a theory that is too abstract and impractical. Most perspectives on leadership clarify and shape thinking about leadership, but few are rooted in or connected to good theory. Almost none are based on research.

A Solid Foundation for Learning Leadership: Experiential Learning Theory and Gestalt Theory and Practice

Experiential Learning Theory

An argument for learning in leadership should stand on a solid foundation of research, theory and practice. Experiential Learning Theory (ELT) draws on the thinking of prominent scholars such as John Dewey, Mary Parker Follett, Paulo Freire, William James, Kurt Lewin, Carl Jung, Jean Piaget, Carl Rogers and Lev Vygotsky to create a theory-based and pragmatic approach to learning. Research in ELT is highly interdisciplinary, addressing learning and education issues in many fields. Studies using ELT have examined aspects of diversity and have been conducted around the world, supporting the cross-cultural applicability of the theory. Biologist James Zull suggests that experiential learning is related to brain functioning. He describes concrete experiences as originating in the sensory cortex, reflective observation coming through the integrative cortex at the back, new abstract concepts occurring in the frontal integrative cortex and active testing involving the motor brain. Figure E shows the brain functions of the four learning modes and the process of learning from experience.

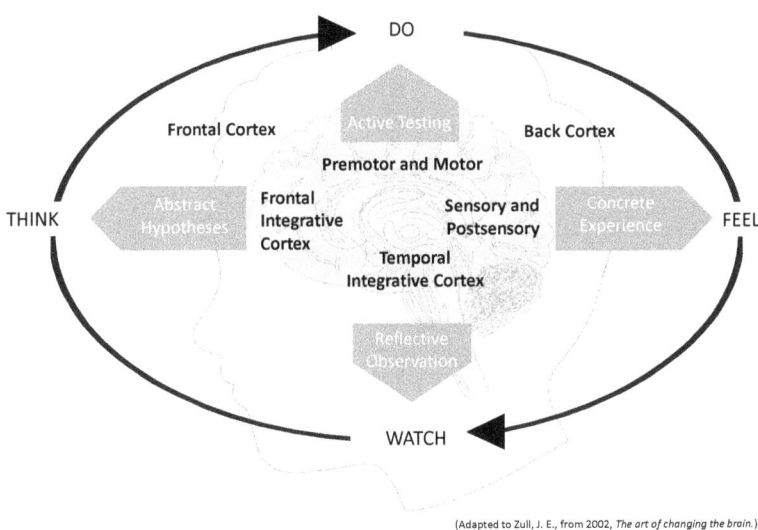

(Adapted to Zull, J. E., from 2002, *The art of changing the brain*.)

Figure E. Neuroscience and Experiential Learning

Basic concepts of ELT – the learning modes, learning cycle, learning styles and learning skills – are used in this book.

The Learning Modes. Four learning modes are involved in learning from experience: concrete experience, reflective observation, abstract conceptualization and active experimentation.

The Learning Cycle. Learning proceeds from the integration of the four learning modes in a cycle that begins with new concrete experiences, moving next to fully and openly reflecting on, observing and considering these experiences from various perspectives in order to create concepts that assimilate these experiences into sound theories so that the theories can be actively tested and applied in life situations (see Figure A).

The Learning Styles. The concept of learning style describes the preferred approach an individual holds for resolving the conflicts between concrete and abstract and between reflection and action. Knowledge of one's preferred style of learning enhances self-awareness and influences the way in which one approaches work, manages emotions and communicates with others. These nine stylistic preferences arise from the patterned ways learners choose between the polarities of experiencing–thinking and reflecting–doing.

1. Initiating style is distinguished by the ability to initiate action to deal with experiences and situations.

2. Experiencing style is distinguished by the ability to find meaning from deep involvement in experience.

3. Creating style is distinguished by the ability to create meaning by observing and reflecting on experiences.

4. Reflecting style is distinguished by the ability to connect experience and ideas through sustained reflection.

5. Analyzing style is distinguished by the ability to integrate and systematize ideas through reflection.

6. Thinking style is distinguished by the capacity for disciplined involvement in abstract reasoning, mathematics and logic.

7. Deciding style is distinguished by the ability to use theories and models to decide on problem solutions and courses of action.

8. Acting style is distinguished by a strong motivation for goal-directed action that integrates people and tasks.

9. Balancing style is distinguished by the ability to flexibly adapt by weighing the pros and cons of acting versus reflecting and experiencing versus thinking.

Gestalt Theory and Practice

Like ELT, Gestalt is a learning perspective. Gestalt practice in organizations results from the convergence of two streams. One stream was inspired by the work of Kurt Lewin that led to the founding of the fields of organization development (OD) and social psychology. Another stream was created by Fritz Perls, Laura Perls, Isadore From and Paul Goodman, founders of Gestalt therapy. From a Gestalt perspective, Lewin provides the theory while Fritz Perls and Laura Perls and their colleagues inform the practice. As a result, Gestalt practitioners have theory to guide *what* they do and principles of practice to know *how* to do it.

Some foundational principles of Gestalt include:[25]

- *Pursue Holism.* Rooted in self-organizing and social constructionist tendencies in human perception, the goal of Gestalt is to seek as full a picture as possible of a given situation.

- *Focus on Process.* Unlike typical intervention approaches, where emphasis is on content and *what* work gets done, Gestalt tilts toward process and *how* work gets done. The task is noticing patterns and emerging themes.

---

25 Summarized from a list of Gestalt principles in Rainey, 2019.

- *Work from Awareness.* Hanafin and Marie-Anne Chidiac portray Gestalt practitioners as "awareness agents" rather than "change agents", while Gestalt scholar and consultant Siminovitch urges development of "awareness IQ". Their sentiments are aligned with the emphasis Gestalt places on consciously knowing in the moment. It is a form of mindful attentiveness that supports the practitioner taking residence in what philosopher Salomon Friedlander describes as the "zone of indifference" or zero point, where complexity, chaos and conflict can best be held. This also allows relaxation of ego and the need 'to get it right'.

- *Bound Awareness.* Shape, organize and configure awareness through the process of bounding to determine how and where to intervene. Boundaries – open or closed, broad or narrow, deep or shallow – influence the strength of connection or 'contact' with self and others.

- *Transform Use-of-self into a Compelling Presence.* Gestalt reframes use-of-self in the concept of 'presence'. Edwin Nevis, renowned teacher of Gestalt and presence, stated that not only does the practitioner stand for and express certain values, attitudes and skills, but they use them in a way to stimulate, and perhaps evoke from the client, action necessary for achieving goals.

- *Use the Cycle of Experience (CoE).* First outlined by Perls in 1947, the CoE is a model for tracking real-time, here-and-now phenomena through a seven-phase cycle that can be applied to a range of experience – personal, coaching, conflict, group or large-scale change.

    o Sensation. Using the senses to gather data about self, others and the environment.

    o Awareness. Noticing emergence of patterns and themes from the sensory data.

o Energy. Tracking energy and interest, or lack thereof, in the patterns and themes.

o Action. Transforming energy, interest and excitement into action.

o Contact. Attending to the shifts and changes that occur as a result of action.

o Closure. Assessing achievements, highlighting learning and celebrating success.

o Withdrawal. Supporting the need for rest, being and renewal.

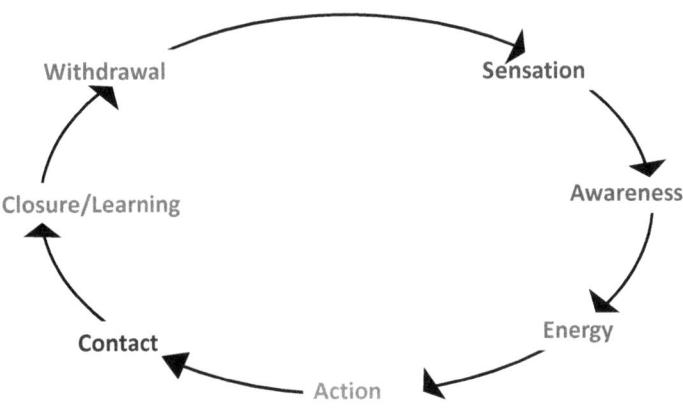

Figure F. The Gestalt Cycle of Experience

- *Follow the Unit of Work (UoW).* While the CoE tracks here-and-now processes, UoW is used to map, design and organize planned change in three simple phases that overlay the CoE:

    o Beginning – determine the work (sensation, awareness)

- o Middle – do the work (mobilization of energy, action, contact)
- o End – close the work (closure, withdrawal).

- *Attend to Resistance.* This refers to forces and factors that are often in conflict with each other. Parties involved see others as resisting their position. Gestalt encourages a holistic stance that is capable of seeing and exploring the "multiple realities".

- *Design Gestalt Experiments.* These are 'on-demand' learning experiences used to stimulate awareness and knowledge. Experiments are co-created by client and practitioner and enacted in the moment to create a 'safe emergency'.

Summary

Strategies of leadership effectiveness come and go with the wind. Success is nothing without learning. At the organizational level, leadership is responsible for learning. This is achieved through the integration of the highly differentiated specialized units. To stay competitive, leaders must manage the internal tension among these specialized units. With the combination of Experiential Learning Theory and Gestalt theory and practice, leaders have established tools for integrating their companies internally so that they can achieve success externally. The RSVP Fundamentals of Leadership Model is an end-to-end framework for continuous learning in a world of continuous change.

PART II

STRATEGIES FOR LEADING IN A LEARNING WAY

Strategies for Leading in a Learning Way

Chapter One has presented the backdrop of the Age of Not Knowing. Chapters Two to Six will discuss in detail the five mastery areas that comprise the *what* and the *how* of leading in a learning way, with skills and practice tips. The four quadrants of *what* leaders do form a clock (see Table 1). Each quadrant consists of three clock positions.

Table 1. The Clock Positions of *What* Leaders Do

Relationship Mastery at eleven, twelve and one o'clock	

Eleven o'clock	Collaborating
Twelve o'clock	Relating
One o'clock	Developing Others

Vision Mastery at two, three and four o'clock	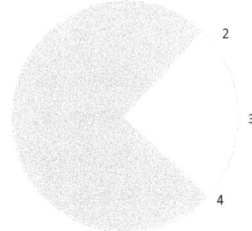

Two o'clock	Creating
Three o'clock	Gathering Information
Four o'clock	Analyzing Information

Strategy Mastery at five, six and seven o'clock

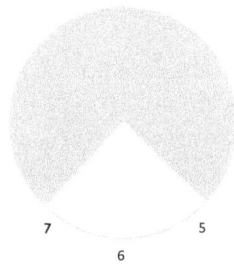

Five o'clock	Organizing
Six o'clock	Planning
Seven o'clock	Managing Technology

Performance Mastery at eight, nine and ten o'clock

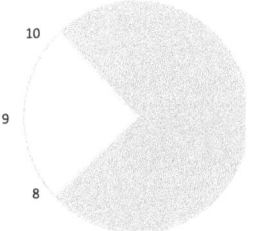

Eight o'clock	Setting Standards
Nine o'clock	Taking Action
Ten o'clock	Innovating

Appendix B is a visual depiction of the RSVP 12 Clock Positions of *What* Leaders Do. Appendix C lists the full set of the 24 skills that comprise *how* leaders do their work. Practice tips for *how* leaders do their work are found in Chapter Six: Presence Mastery.

CHAPTER TWO

Relationship Mastery

re·la·tion·ship / rəˈlāSH(ə)nˌSHip

noun

- the state of having a special connection
- the way in which two or more people, concepts or things are connected and behave toward each other
- a mutual bond between two or more people

We feel 'related' when we feel at one with another (person or object) in some heartfelt way.

Helen Harris Perlman, renowned relationship scholar[26]

Relationship Mastery is the ability of leaders to build relationships with stakeholders of their organization, both internally and externally. In this chapter, we look at events that elevated the importance of relationships at work and how, in the current environment, leaders who build positive relationships are better positioned to increase the followership necessary for their companies to excel. We explore the many configurations of people that leaders must engage (such as individuals, groups and organizations) and some of the many

26 See Perlman, 1979, p. 23.

supplemental roles they must assume (e.g., mentor, coach, ally, partner, networker). Building trust, creating psychological safety, facilitating dialogue, listening actively and managing boundaries are identified as conditions conducive to fostering productive relationships. The learning skills and behaviors necessary for developing Relationship Mastery are included. This chapter concludes with a summary.

Introduction

Existentially, we may feel as though we are navigating the world alone, but functionally, we are interdependent beings, relying on one another for support and guidance. Interacting with others helps to sustain and advance the human condition. As one of the principal contexts of our lives, relationships shape our identity, provide a sense of belonging and spark our affection for one another. In the opening quote, Helen Perlman explains that being related tugs at the heart and stirs emotions. She adds this poignant description of what it is like to be connected:

> Relationship is a human being's feeling or sense of emotional bonding with another. It leaps into being like an electric current, or it emerges and develops cautiously when emotion is aroused by and invested in someone or something and that someone or something 'connects back' responsively. We feel 'related' when we feel at one with another (person or object) in some heartfelt way.[27]

The potency of special relationships is something we all have experienced. It is hard to imagine not having that childhood buddy with whom we shared secrets of our misdeeds and first love, or what life today would be without close friends to rejoice with us in our success and encourage us in our sorrows. It is easy to make the case that we are social beings regardless of claims of introversion or extraversion.

[27] Perlman, 1979, p. 23.

Relating with others is also a core part of organizational life. Many of us have 'partners in crime' at work whom we trust to share our perception of our manager and office gossip, and have a mentor who gets us back on track with one word of advice. People are the primary reason that work gets done in organizations. It is through human connections that organizational culture is created and maintained. The quality of these connections contributes to personal well-being, a sense of safety, and productivity. This social constructionist perspective is an affirmation that organizational effectiveness is influenced as much or more by people and their experience with each other as it is driven by technical factors. And leaders play a pivotal role in leveraging the power of people at work. For this reason, we position Relationship Mastery as the first fundamental of the RSVP Model.

Relationships require social sensitivity and the effort of all parties involved. But extra effort is required of those who lead. We can assign a myriad of characteristics to the role of the leader, but at the most basic level, leadership is a social function where the leader connects with and influences others, and, in turn, is influenced by them. The case for fostering relationships at work has never been more urgent. Those at the top are literally learning on the run, more dependent on employees for knowledge as change and novel challenges become daily occurrences. Oddly, while most of us recognize that people are indispensable at work, their importance is not always reflected in practice. A look back at the beginning of organizational theory and practice may help to understand why this is the case.

The Year They Discovered People

> The point of view which gradually emerged from the [Hawthorne] studies was to regard a business organization as a social system.
>
> Donald Chipman, former Hawthorne studies observer, 1977

CHAPTER TWO

Throughout this book, we indicate that the human or people side of work was a late consideration in the early designs of organizations. Influenced in great part by the 1911 publication of Frederick Taylor's *Principles of Scientific Management*, meeting the needs of employees became secondary to organizational performance. Companies placed their bets on solving problems and efficiency of production.[28] Without question, scientific management made a big contribution to the transition from the agricultural society to the industrial society and continues to inform management and leadership theory and practice, but it did not allow much space for supporting employees. Managerial standards rarely assigned importance to the needs of those executing the tasks; instead, guidelines advanced the assumption that employees were motivated primarily by monetary rewards. Those doing the work were expected to do their job, appreciate getting paid and be happy. And to ensure compliance, managers kept their distance. They were impersonal.

1924

Things took a turn in 1924 when the National Academy of Science started an experiment in Chicago with Western Electric, at their Hawthorne Works, and three other companies. The aim was to determine how lighting affected employee performance. Researchers hypothesized that if lighting increased in work areas, output would improve. Findings revealed that, for sure, output went up with more lighting. But output also rose when lights had not been changed, and output continued to increase even when lights were turned down. Perplexed, scientists called off the study. But luckily, Western Electric decided to conduct another round of research, except, this time, without their previous research partners. Changes in the design allowed workers to take breaks, work different hours and give feedback about their experience. A significant breakthrough occurred. Reasons for the increase in productivity involved employees working together in a group, feeling special due to working in a

---

28 See Chapter One, Section C: Understanding Leadership.

room separated from other employees, and having a sympathetic supervisor. What mattered were the social connections among the workers and with their supervisor. The research is regarded as the first scientific inquiry into employee attitudes and socialization at work. Donald Chipman, an observer in the study, remarked that it was the year companies discovered people.[29]

The Hawthorne studies were a major factor in spotlighting the psychological and sociological (psycho-social) aspects of employee behavior. They opened the door to the view of business settings as social systems. Further confirmation came in the 1950s when the Human Relations movement took hold in the USA at the NTL Institute for Applied Behavioral Science and Stanford University, and in the UK at the Tavistock Institute. Individuals, many of them managers and leaders, enrolled in workshops to increase their self-awareness and knowledge of human interactions.

Relationships and Emotional Intelligence

In 1995, psychologist Daniel Goleman put a pragmatic face on relationships at work with the publication of his article 'Emotional Intelligence'. Goleman, a psychologist, positioned emotional intelligence (EQ) at the center of effective leadership and identified four overarching components: self-awareness, self-management, awareness of others and relationship management. According to Goleman, EQ makes a measurable difference in leader and follower bottom-line performance. His findings are supported in independent research around the globe. A 2013 study by David Zes and Dana Landis of the Korn Ferry Institute that focused on the US stock market performance of 486 publicly traded companies revealed that self-awareness is critical to career success and improved executive leadership. Just as notable were findings showing a correlation between self-awareness and overall company financial performance. There

---

29 See the 1974 AT&T video about the research, aptly entitled *The Year They Discovered People*. For more details about the Hawthorne studies, see *Management and the Worker* (Roethlisberger and Dickson, 1939).

are indications that public companies with a higher rate of financial return hire professionals with higher levels of EQ. Another 2004 study by Fred Luthans and Suzanne Peterson showed that leaders with higher self-awareness not only have greater job satisfaction and commitment to their employer, but the effect trickles down to their direct reports. Martyn Newman's research in 2017 indicated that the adaptive skills needed in organizations are rooted in emotional and social behaviors. Newman, a clinical psychologist, stated that when EQ grows among individuals in a company, levels of absenteeism drop, creativity goes up and engagement increases.

Relating to Self

Being connected to others begins with a good grounding in sense of self. According to Rainey and Jones, understanding self includes self-awareness, self-concept, self-esteem and social-self. Self-acceptance, self-reliance, self-care and self-love are added to the list that we provide to leaders in their exploration of their relationship with themselves.

- *Self-awareness.* Getting to *know* who you are – your personal values and sense of ethics, assumptions, biases, who and what you like and dislike, your tendencies, strengths, weaknesses, cultural background and the broader context of your life.

- *Self-concept.* Gaining a good sense of how you *think* about yourself, who you believe you are, how you construct your identity and seeking feedback from others about their perceptions of you.

- *Self-esteem.* Determining how you *feel* about yourself, the level of value and worth that you assign to yourself. Uncovering what triggers good and bad feelings about your worth and developing strategies to manage your 'mood' elevator.

- *Social-self.* Working on your *relatability*. Being clear about how you relate to others both in your personal and professional lives. Developing relationships that are built on mutual support where you and others treat each other well. Avoiding selfishness and destructive narcissism.

- *Self-acceptance. Coming to terms* with your attributes, positive and negative. Developing the ability to protect yourself from negative criticism and being comfortable with receiving positive feedback.

- *Self-reliance.* Being first a support and best friend to yourself. Developing a healthy *dependence on yourself* and being confident with self-counsel. Trusting your gut. Believing you will be okay during tough times and crises. Being optimistic.

- *Self-care.* Prioritizing *good health* and ensuring well-being. Getting sufficient sleep, nutrition, rest and recreation. Spending time alone – meditating, journaling and practicing yoga. Being with nature. Pursuing hobbies. Continuously learning.

- *Self-love.* Loving you. Allowing yourself to *marvel at yourself*, to think highly of yourself. Dispensing with self-shaming. Enjoying being who you are even on your worst days. Celebrating you.

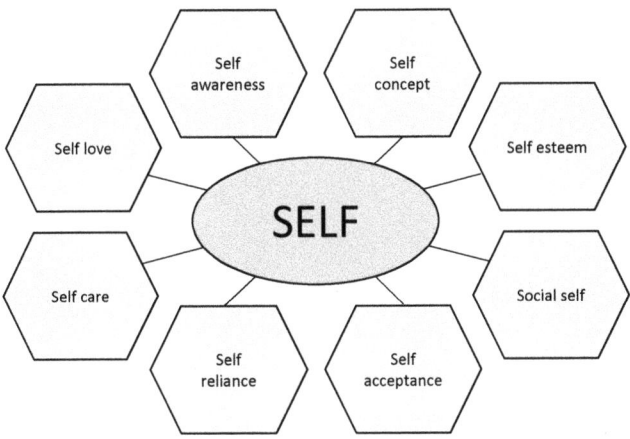

Figure G. Key Factors of Relating to Self

Relating to Others

It makes good business sense for leaders to demonstrate concern for issues affecting employees, customers and the broader community, in part because those issues will ultimately impact the organization and in part because it is the right thing to do as a contributing member of society. Relating to others consists of the leader interacting with others in multiple social configurations and in multiple roles.

The Social Configurations of Relating

- *Individual.* The focus is on one person, their feelings, thoughts, behavior, aspirations.

- *Interpersonal.* The focus is on the relationship between the leader and one other individual, or the leader and other groupings of individuals.

- *Group/Team.* The focus is on the group or team as a social entity and its functioning.

- *Department/Division.* The focus is on clearly bounded and defined sub areas of the company and their functioning.

- *Organization.* The focus is on the enterprise as a whole and the integrated, interdependent and appropriately independent operation of its subsystems.

- *Largest system.* The focus is on the interdependent functioning of internal (company) and external environments and their subsystems.

The Leadership Roles of Relating

- *Coach.* With so many executive coaches in the market, a leader may well wonder why they should be involved in coaching. The leader-as-coach is not about leveraging strengths and tracking achievement of developmental goals for the next year. Rather, it is about what is happening right now; what is emerging for individuals and teams that cannot wait to be rescued by Human Resources or until the next meeting with an executive coach. Whether it is extracting ideas, being a sounding board or giving advice, the leader-as-coach is a necessary role.

- *Mentor.* Leaders possess a wealth of experience and knowledge that is beneficial to the growth and development of those coming behind them. Mentoring has proved to be an effective form of leadership development. It is cost effective, customized to the mentee and builds relationships. The leader-as-mentor helps their mentee expand their skills, make better decisions, navigate the cultural dynamics of the company and gain new perspectives on life and career. Mentees get a sounding board and someone to provide advice and counsel. They also have access to an alternative reality of organizational life, something many top leaders value knowing (reverse/reciprocal mentoring). Most mentees grow up to be mentors themselves.

- *Team Builder.* Building an effective team is one of the first orders of business for leaders, and there are many courses and experts to assist in the job of understanding group process and team dynamics. In the meantime, leaders can do a few things on their own that will make a huge difference. Assemble a competent and diverse team. Once assembled, learn to 'read the room'. This involves listening, noticing, recognizing patterns of behavior, and deciding when and how to surface observations. Soon, members of the team will emulate the leader's behavior.

- *Ally and Advocate.* This involves actively advocating and intervening on behalf of individuals and groups that have been adversely impacted by systemic structures, processes and ways of working. The leader-as-ally sends the message that everyone belongs and will be treated equally.

- *Conflict Manager.* Managing relationships often places leaders in very tense situations. Think of former United States Senator George Mitchell to get an idea of what it takes to be a relationship master in the eye of a storm. Mitchell is credited as the architect of the 1998 Good Friday Agreement that ended decades of civil war between Catholics and Protestants in Northern Ireland. Mitchell was described as out-listening everyone. He respected all sides of the issue. Ninety percent of the role of the leader as Conflict Manager consists of doing what George Mitchell did: making room for all points of view.

- *Convener of Community.* We define community as the largest social system that consists of internal and external stakeholders. The idea of convening community comes from Peter Block who, in his 2008 *T+D* Journal article 'Leadership and the small group', points out that we must understand that the future resides in the spaces that we occupy. The room is what we want to create, right now. Block insists that there is no need to wait for the future – that the way we structure how we come together is as critical as the issue that we come to address.

- *Customer Liaison.* The leader interacts with customers to share the company's values, vision and priorities, and to express appreciation for their contribution to its success.

- *Business Partner.* This involves cooperating with others to advance mutual support. The partnership can be for personal or professional gain and may be formed with individuals, colleagues, investors, other firms, and aspects and agencies of the external environment such as the government, education and the local community.

- *Networker.* This is often for the purpose of career development, where leaders interact with individuals and participate in groups both inside and outside of their respective field of expertise and industry. Conferences are a way leaders learn from each other, provide mutual support and exchange information. The Legatum Leadership Forum convenes leaders annually to network, learn and be a support for each other. Those in attendance describe their time together as 'a cure for CEO loneliness'.[30]

Conditions Conducive to Building Relationships

Relationships are difficult and come with unique challenges when leaders are involved. Building trust, creating psychological safety, facilitating dialogue, active listening and managing boundaries are conditions conducive to making interactions more effective.

Building Trust

Relationships thrive in a climate of trust. When we hear someone say they have a best friend, it is safe to assume that that relationship is built on trust. A good working environment is one where employees trust the organization, trust each other and, foremost, trust the leadership. When leaders are perceived as fair, ethical and reliable, there is less worry about the reputation and future of the company. The attention of employees remains focused on work. Conversely, lack of credibility, appearance of bias, and unethical and criminal behavior all lead to a lack of trust in leadership.

In his research on the neuroscience of trust, Paul Zak, a professor of economics, psychology and management at Claremont Graduate University, learned that trust is associated with economic performance.

> Compared with people at low-trust companies, people at high-trust companies report: 74% less stress, 106% more energy at work, 50% higher productivity, 13% fewer sick days, 76% more engagement, 29% more satisfaction with their lives, 40% less burnout.[31]

30 The Legatum Leadership Forum is an annual four-day event that convenes the CEOs from across Legatum's philanthropic and commercial investments (approximately 15 people). During these four days, the leaders discuss challenges they face, external speakers share relevant leadership ideas and experience, and the group builds relationship through extraordinary shared experiences.
31 Zak, 2017a, pp. 4–5.

For most people, developing trust in others takes time; however, losing trust can happen almost instantaneously. To lead for trust, Zak advises leaders to set clear direction, provide resources for employees to work productively, and *trust* them to do their work autonomously.

Creating Psychological Safety

Most employees welcome the opportunity to forge a relationship with their leaders – to get to know them and find out more about the company, to learn from them, experience their presence or simply just 'hang out' with them. But employees are guarded in the presence of leadership if they do not feel psychologically safe. A study by Harvard professor Amy Edmondson defines psychological safety in teams as the shared belief held by team members that it is safe to take risks. In a psychologically safe environment, individuals feel that they can offer alternative viewpoints, ask questions and disclose concerns without the threat of retaliation or reprimand. A 2015 study of 200 employees by Google's People Operations identified five attributes that distinguish good teams from other teams at the company: psychological safety, dependability, structure and clarity, meaning of work, and the impact of work on the employee. Of the five attributes, psychological safety ranked as most important by a wide margin. The researchers concluded that psychological safety is the foundation of effective teamwork. Standards of conduct are useful in ensuring an environment where everyone feels safe to express themselves without reprimand or reprisals.

Facilitating Dialogue

> We have cast our own lot with learning, and learning will pull us through. But this learning must be reimbued with the texture and feeling of human experiences shared and interpreted through dialogue with each other.
>
> David Kolb[32]

---

32 Kolb, 2015, p. 2.

Dialogue is sustained conversation that promotes creativity and problem solving, and elevates learning. Providing a forum for dialogue is one of the most proactive gestures leaders can do to enhance relationships at work. With dialogue, leaders add human experience to the context of the organization. Ideas are shared, considered, challenged and built upon. Broader horizons result from this 'fusion of horizons' – situating one possibility next to other possibilities. In the process, people get the opportunity to experience each other more fully beyond the typical roles they occupy in the company, and relationships grow.

Additional merits of dialogue are found in its practicality, its ability to weaken totalitarianism and its cathartic qualities. According to Paulo Freire, renowned educator and philosopher, dialogue is key to the emancipation of those who are oppressed. Dialogue plays a role in identity formation. When individuals react and respond to each other, their knowledge of who they are and what they value becomes more apparent. Moreover, each party gets to know the other and recognizes the identity of the other. Understanding individual identity and the identities of others leads to seeing more similarity than difference.

Dialogue is most effective when parties listen to each other across boundaries of difference. Ideal listening along with making space for those who speak in a 'different voice' are necessary components of good conversation. Awareness of the tone of connection is critical. And leaders must monitor what is referred to as the 'slow creep' of hierarchy, which can easily make its way into conversations among individuals of different rank. Caution must be applied against conversation stoppers and people who engage in monologues. A suitable tone of conversation advances dialogue. However, it is not the goal to suppress passion or promote a false congeniality, but to foster deeper connections. Guidelines of participation, ideally developed by the parties involved, establish boundaries of behavior.

In the era of social networks, technology has become a critical player in relationship building. Leaders use technology to connect virtually, build faster and more informed responses to pressing matters, and include a broader array of constituents in conversations. Immediate connections can be made, including those beyond traditional sources (employees, experts, competitors, suppliers), to gather data, seek opinions and engage with people in remote parts of the world. Though dialogue on social platforms is relatively new, organizations are becoming skilled in starting and facilitating conversations. Asking questions, using visuals and taking polls are great conversation starters. Using functions such as chat to collect data that can be mined in break-out groups or in plenary is proving surprisingly effective.

Active Listening

The ability to listen is fundamental to good dialogue. Often equated with hearing, listening is mistakenly regarded as passive, and thus neglected. In truth, listening does involve hearing, but they are not the same. Hearing is the act of perceiving sound by the ear. If one is not hard of hearing, then hearing is a natural part of sensory functioning. On the other hand, listening is a conscious act – something we choose to do. Listening requires concentration so that our brains can process the meaning of the words, sentences and sounds we hear. When leaders learn to listen, they realize how hopeless they have been as listeners.

Create an Environment for Great Conversation. If the conversation is important, do not leave the setting to chance. Place and space are important components of relationship building and interpersonal engagement. Consider where and when conversations should occur.

Ask Powerful Questions. Productive conversations are stimulated by good questions. If there is interest in getting more information, then the best kind of question should be used – open, closed or leading. Open-ended questions are best for igniting thoughts and feelings.

Make Powerful Statements. Conversations that solely rely on questions feel one-sided and leave the other party with a feeling of being interrogated. *Remember, there is always a thought behind every question.* Consider stepping back and connecting with the thought that precedes the question.

Listen to Silence. Good conversations benefit from moments of silence when the parties engage each other without speaking. This provides a different form of listening. It is a non-directed, interpersonal state of being. When conversation is rushed or cluttered with too much talking and too many words, affection is pushed to the side. True connection is held hostage. Slowing down and savoring the moment is outright spiritual.

Leaders should balance powerful questions, powerful statements, silence and movement in their conversation. They should share thoughts, opinions and perspectives, and be open to listening to others. Good conversations are characterized by:

1. Giving and getting information
2. Inquiring about others and disclosing about self
3. Providing support (blanket) and challenge (sandpaper).[33]

Listen to Yourself. We support leaders listening to themselves as they speak. It is challenging at first, but it can be done. Do they speak without pausing or taking a deep breath? Do they provide an explanation or give an example without determining if one is needed? Do they speak in a monotone that is void of voice inflection? The first step in good listening is listening. Table 2 provides tips for good listening.

Boundary Management

Relating is a live, organic and unpredictable process where anything can happen. Managing boundaries of rank, role and space is critical. Inappropriate comments are a violation of boundaries and leave everyone feeling uncomfortable, if not downright unsafe. Physical

---

[33] 'Sandpaper and blanket' is a concept we learned at the NTL Institute.

Table 2. Tips for Good Listening

- Anchor yourself with good breathing.
- Maintain respectable boundaries: when face to face, keep a comfortable physical distance; when virtual, do not constantly lean into the screen.
- Do not allow your body language to impact the free flow of conversation. When virtual, manage distractions and movements that might suggest you are not attentive, such as looking side to side, or staring away.
- Create a natural pace and rhythm to the conversation – not too fast, not too slow, not too late.
- Show interest in the speaker.
- Talk about yourself but not too much, not too soon.
- Exercise patience. Do not constantly interrupt.
- Do not condemn or patronize.
- Practice subtle acknowledgements such as occasional nodding of the head.
- Be involved but not intense. Total silence, fixed staring and overplayed compassion are disconcerting.
- Listen with all your senses. Do not hamper yourself by only focusing on what you hear and discounting what you feel, see, smell and taste.
- Practice listening from both your *heart* (appreciation and empathy) and with your *head* (comprehension, discernment and judgment).
- Trust your gut and intuition.
- Do not be a 'gotcha' listener, looking for ways to entrap the speaker.
- Be an intentional listener. Timing and tone are critical. Know when to agree and when to disagree, and when to tell a story about yourself rather than listening to the speaker's story.
- Learn to listen to yourself while listening to others.

boundaries must be respected when face to face. A friendly touch is an intrusion if uninvited. Typical questions about managing boundaries include: Where is the line? How close is too close? How open is too open? How personal? In the office, relationships come with the agony and the ecstasy of human experience. More intimate relationships can produce, as historical novelist, poet and playwright Sir Walter Scott described, "tangled webs". In these cases, it becomes difficult to discern whether a promotion or pay increase is based on objectivity or favoritism. The opposite happens as well. Denial of opportunities once the relationship ends arouses suspicion. Ethical guidelines help leaders and employees understand the boundaries of relationships at work.

Relationship Inquiry

Relationship, Vision, Strategy and Performance involve asking and answering questions that inform leadership decisions. We have assembled a set of questions that are useful prompts for leadership in Relationship Mastery. The questions are as important as the answers. Most of the questions have been used in many organizations and proven to be effective. They are strong benchmarks for reflection. A constantly changing environment and company performance may warrant additional or different questions that are unique to a particular business situation. A diverse and inclusive pool of participants add value through the questions they ask, the assumptions they challenge, as well as the answers they provide. Revisiting and refreshing the questions is as vital as updating the answers.

Questions of Relationship Inquiry

1. What is the make-up of our top leadership team?
2. How are we staying connected to our employees in ways that make them feel valued?

3. To what extent do we interact with our external stakeholders (e.g., investors, customers, suppliers, regulators, the broader community)?

4. What is our strategy for growth through partnerships, alliances or collaborations within and outside our industry?

5. How do we keep our skills, capabilities, capacity and technology up to date and aligned?

6. What is our development plan to recruit, develop and retain a diverse workforce?

7. How do we plan to educate our company and change our culture if needed, based on our commitment to diversity, equity and inclusion?

8. What is the current state of our succession plan – long term and in the event of an emergency?

Skills of Relationship Mastery

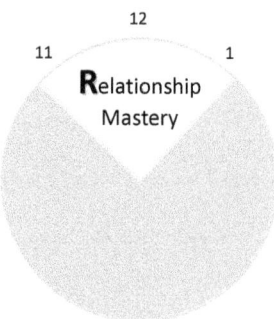

Concrete Experience is the mode of learning for Relationship Mastery with Interpersonal Skills located in the northern quadrant: Collaborating at eleven o'clock, Relating at twelve o'clock and Developing Others at one o'clock (Table 3). Each clock position consists of three items.

Table 3. Relationship Mastery

Learning Style: Concrete Experience

Quadrant: Interpersonal Skills

Eleven o'clock: Collaborating

    11:00 Building a leadership team

    11:20 Building community

    11:40 Promoting partnerships and alliances

Twelve o'clock: Relating

    12:00 Interacting with awareness of self, others and the environment

    12:20 Building trusting relationships

    12:40 Communicating effectively

One o'clock: Developing Others

    01:00 Mentoring, motivating and inspiring others

    01:20 Giving and receiving feedback

    01:40 Empathizing

Eleven o'clock: Collaborating

11:00 Building a leadership team

Most of the work in organizations is done in groups. Every team is a group, but every group is not a team. Teams are not built by appointment alone. The leader must deliberately develop them. The intentional effort pays off in improved processes and better outcomes. An integrated leadership team committed to what is best for the enterprise outperforms a collection of individuals who are dedicated to improving their personal performance or the performance of their unit. The difference is alignment, shared goals, clear roles, self-sustaining processes and commitment to mutual success. Alignment, synergy, efficiency and a sense of belonging are the primary payoffs of good teamwork. The whole is not automatically greater than the sum of the parts. It is the leader's responsibility to ensure that the collective performance exceeds the aggregate of the individual members.

11:20 Building community

Teams exist in a larger community of an organization, which exists in a larger community of markets, industries, neighborhoods and nations. Communities of family and society are part of the relational ecosystem within which organizations exist. Leaders have an opportunity and a responsibility to create positive relationships among all stakeholders. Community action to build fellowship between the organization and its environment benefits all constituents. Convening community is a crucial leadership skill and empowerment strategy. It is efficient in that a broader span of citizens participates in identifying common objectives. Conversations in small groups give birth to friendships and collaborations that often endure. This form of large-system relationship building relies on additional leaderships skills such as creating psychological safety, listening, facilitating dialogue, listening, empathizing, and giving and seeking feedback.

11:40 Promoting partnerships and alliances

Leaders model the collaborative spirit when they work with others at the level of partnerships and alliances. Partnering has proven successful in leveraging the best of the parties involved through mergers and other strategic combinations. They deliver assurance and a sense that 'we are in this together'. Taking the lead in forming partnerships and alliances enhances the organization's profile. The skills involved in forging joint ventures include seeing commonalities, optimism and an ability to negotiate. Enrolling others to come together and create together for mutual benefit represents a risk (of rejection or losing advantage) and necessitates the presentation of a compelling case for achieving common goals. Skilled leaders create a functioning coalition ranging from soulmates to strange bedfellows.

Twelve o'clock: Relating

12:00 *Interacting with awareness of self, others and the environment*

The capacity for self-awareness is uniquely human and represents the greatest difference between humans and other species. This skill includes the ability to sense and experience fully as a human being, to reflect on that experience and extract meaning that informs the need to adapt. Self-aware leaders pay attention to and take responsibility for the impact their words and behavior have on others. They realize when meeting someone for the first time that it takes only a few seconds to form a first and lasting impression. Self-aware leaders know that they may not always achieve the impact they hope for. They are curious about their impact and meet disconnects with curiosity rather than defensiveness. Learning leaders take time regularly to scan what is happening inside themselves and around them. They are interested in others and the environment, putting forth effort to engage and relate to both.

12:20 *Building trusting relationships*

Building trust ranks high as a leadership competency. No aspect of the leader's enduring effectiveness demands more than trust. Trust is a variable in every equation of leadership, followership, high performance, change management and teamwork. Developing trusting relationships takes patience and persistence. The skills involved include being open, taking risks, personal integrity, congruence, consistency, reliability and the ability to speak the truth. Trust travels both ways: employees need to trust leaders, and leaders must trust their employees. Margaret Hamilton was a NASA systems engineer programmer on the Apollo 11 mission. Flight Director Gene Kranz completely trusted her work in the crucial moments when Apollo 11 was landing on the moon. When an alarm went off, Gene Kranz had to decide instantly whether to abort the landing or not. It was a choice between this alarm and his confidence in her work. He trusted her and ignored the alarm. The Eagle landed, with 30 seconds of thruster capability left. Hamilton was awarded the United States Medal of Freedom. So was Kranz. When leaders lose the trust of their followers, they are finished. Even harder than building trust is rebuilding inherited mistrust.

12:40 Communicating effectively

Swedish telecommunications firm Ericsson displayed in the lobby of its world headquarters these words: "It's about communication between people, the rest is just technology". True connection with the audience is far superior to a PowerPoint presentation. Communication skills in a leader go beyond style. Effective communication is at least as much about listening as it is speaking. Listening with discernment cultivates greater awareness. This involves engaging people in a way that meets them where they are, not where the speaker is or would like them to be. It is about a way of exchanging so both parties feel heard and respected. Listening skills for the RSVP leader include data gathering using *powerful questions*. Great questions can contribute more to performance improvement than great answers. But communication is interpersonal and also consists of *powerful statements*. Leaders learn much more listening to others than to themselves. They need to be able to: tell a story people can relate to; invite, take in and consider a disparate, even hostile, set of viewpoints; convey what is on their mind and in their heart; and be genuinely interested in someone else's experience.

One o'clock: Developing Others

1:00 Mentoring, motivating and inspiring others

Leaders never succeed alone. They must contribute to the development of others. Mentoring is a way for leaders to 'pay it forward' by sharing experience, learning, and providing advice and counsel. Mentors often see promise in their mentees that their mentees may not yet see in themselves. This belief beyond evidence sparks self-confidence. Whether it takes a team or a village, the ability to elevate followers' spirit and commitment is often the difference between success and failure. Leaders wear many hats but they also motivate and inspire. The difference between motivation and inspiration is the source. Leaders motivate when they give others a reason to do their job, while workers are inspired when they have the internal drive to want to do their job. Motivation comes from without. Inspiration comes from within. Relationship masters motivate others by being a role model of ethical behavior, by treating others with respect and by keeping their promises to customers. Inspiration usually follows. Other leaders are inspired and want to emulate them. The greatest thing a leader can develop is other leaders.

1:20 Giving and receiving feedback

Being a role model is one of the two powerful development tools at a leader's disposal. The other is giving feedback that matters. Feedback nourishes growth. It is a necessary component of rapid adaptation to a changing environment. Feedback is a process, not an event, suggesting that it is on-going when needed. Good feedback is delivered in a way that captivates and elevates rather than deflates and discourages. It must be clear and sharp in order to induce reflection and consideration. Powerful feedback is data which intentionally and precisely targets the edges of the receiver's comfort zone. Well-crafted feedback provokes disruption, invites exploration and conveys confidence. As a role model, the leader themself seeks feedback as a source for continuous personal improvement. Former

New York City Mayor Ed Koch was famous for regularly asking his constituents "How am I doing?"

1:40 Empathizing

Empathy has been shown to be positively related to job performance. The empathetic leader appreciates the needs of others even if they have never experienced the same thing. Full understanding may not be possible when someone has lost their home but appreciating the circumstances of losing something very valuable is empathetic. Technically, empathy is not 'walk a mile in my shoes'. It is recalling when you have walked a similar path in similar shoes. Empathy is an intentional form of caring, and that caring must be experienced as authentic. Still, empathizing does not preclude making difficult decisions. Empathy is also treating others with respect regardless of the difficulty of the decision or engagement. In the words of the poet Maya Angelou, "People will forget what you said, people will forget what you did, but people will never forget how you made them feel". The human aspect of relating is in full effect in empathy.

Relationship Mastery Usage Indicator

We have discussed how the Relationship Mastery skills are expressed and developed. Table 4 is a summary of the skills when well-used, under-used and over-used.

Table 4. The Relationship Mastery Usage Indicator

Skill Area	Well-used	Under-used	Over-used
Eleven o'clock Collaborating	Interactions characterized by co-creation, and collaboration; requires mindset of 'we need' more than 'I want'; knowing when to lead and when to manage; being inclusive.	Over-reliance on individuals and stars and those who behave and think like the leader; failing to align elements of the organization's ecosystem to avoid working at cross purposes.	'Group think'; reluctance to take individual action when warranted; assuming that every situation requires a group of collaborators; excessive use of consensus decision making.
Twelve o'clock Relating	Interacting with a full range of stakeholders; listening, acknowledging, considering others; assuming others have ideas to contribute and you have something to learn; being authentic in caring.	Interacting within a limited scope of centralized power; seeking input and never using it; scripted rather than authentic exchanges with stakeholders; unbalanced attention internally or externally.	Over-reliance on delegation; too much stakeholder input; excessive scanning at the expense of execution; lack of boundaries of confidentiality and privacy.
One o'clock Developing Others	Developing a fair and equitable pay/performance system; balancing learning and performance; utilizing training, mentoring and coaching; including career development in development strategy; using both internal and external resources.	Failure to upgrade skills, capability and capacity to meet today's work requirements and adapt to the latest technology; no succession plan; lack of sensitivity to the developmental needs of diverse candidates.	Constant shifting of roles; Placing employees in positions beyond their expertise, without support; too much developmental oversight; unhealthy dependence on tools and techniques versus learning from experience.

CHAPTER TWO

Summary

This chapter discussed the importance of people in organizations and their relationships with each other and with leaders. Never have relationships been so critical to the success of organizations. New ways of working are dependent upon knowledge from all areas of the company. It is through relationships that work gets done, friendships and alliances are born, people get support and careers are advanced. The work of the leader in Relationship Mastery is accomplished by engaging with multiple configurations of stakeholders in different roles. But the job of relating begins with the leader relating to their self. Psychological safety, dialogue, listening and boundary management constitute a solid foundation for good leadership to cultivate trusting relationships.

Relationship Mastery is the quadrant of the *Concrete Experience* Learning Style. On the Leadership Skills Profile (LSP), Relationship involves the following sets of *Interpersonal Skills*:

- Collaborating (eleven o'clock)
- Relating (twelve o'clock)
- Developing others (one o'clock).

CHAPTER THREE

Vision Mastery

vi·sion / viZHən

noun

- foresight, intuition, perception, perspective, discernment
- the ability to see beyond the obvious
- an experience in which a personage, thing or event appears vividly or credibly to the mind, although not actually present

If you don't know where you're going, you'll probably end up somewhere else.

Yogi Berra, baseball manager

For visibility, these days, seems to somehow equate to success. Do not be afraid to disappear from it, from us for a while and see what comes to you in the silence.

Michaela Coel, writer and performer

Vision Mastery is the leadership process that delivers an image of what a company aspires to and believes it can become. When most effective, the outcome is clarity of direction, esprit de corps among stakeholders and arrival at the desired destination. A vision often is accompanied by a purpose and a mission. In this chapter, we define vision, purpose and mission and discuss their relationship to each other. Guidelines for preparing a vision statement are presented, beginning with slowing down and being available for reflection. Also included are the skills and behaviors necessary for developing Vision Mastery. This chapter concludes with a summary.

Introduction

Organizations suffer in the absence of direction. It is leadership that establishes the way forward with a vision – the 'north star' that keeps the company aligned and members moving along the same path. The vision is the overarching guide for Strategy Mastery and Performance Mastery. Though the quote from sports legend Yogi Berra is familiar and found in many writings about leadership, we include it here because it so effectively drives home the message that leaders must know and communicate where they are steering the business. Members of a firm should not be left wondering if they should flip a coin to decide which road to take. Vision Mastery involves leaders gaining perspective. But leadership is a high-demand job and achieving the focus needed to expand perspective is difficult. Michaela Coel underscores the benefit of reflection in discerning one's point of view. As part of her acceptance speech for her 2021 Emmy, the artist spoke passionately about the rewards that flow from stillness. In very pragmatic terms, and with a dose of humor, Berra offers leaders a rationale for a vision while Coel ushers them into the unfamiliar territory of slowing down as a creative resource. Fellow award-winning artist and creator of acclaimed musicals, *Hamilton* and *In the Heights*, Lin-Manuel Miranda agrees with Coel when he says, "But something that helps me make sense of stuff – because I'm not actually a good multitasker – is that I need the space to daydream and space out on the thing that is in front of me."[34] Harvard

---

34 Cole Rachel, 2022.

professor Abraham Zaleznik[35] believes that vision is the hallmark of leadership, less a derivative of spreadsheets and more a product of the imagination that is brought to bear on the growth of a company.

Visionaries transform the world with their hopes and dreams. Humanitarians and social activists readily come to mind because, by nature, they are counter-cultural in their assumptions about the way things should and could be. They imagine a different world and commit their lives to pursuing their ideals, often working on behalf of the greater good. Most of us are familiar with the efforts of Malala Yousafzai, Mother Theresa and Oskar Schindler. But society breeds a fine assortment of visionaries. Think of computer scientist Tim Berners-Lee, physicist and chemist Marie Curie, entrepreneur Madam C.J. Walker, Twitter co-creators Evan Williams, Christopher Isaac Stone and Jack Dorsey, and fashion designers Miuccia Prada and Ralph Lauren. Leaders of nations are great visionaries. In 2010, the United Arab Emirates (UAE)[36] launched an ambitious vision to make the UAE one of the best countries in the world by the Golden Jubilee of the Union in 2021. By all accounts, that vision was translated into reality. Today, UAE, a true oasis in the desert, is one of the most popular destinations for tourism, business, investment and citizenship. When we think of UAE, we are reminded of the words of playwright George Bernard Shaw: "Some men see things as they are and say 'why?' – I dream of things that never were and say 'why not?'"

In the role of visionary, the leader is, at all times, a systems thinker, mindful of the enterprise in its entirety and the forces impacting it. Regardless of where they sit in the company – middle, bottom or top – leaders dangle on a precipice, seeking a full account of what is going on. Dominic Barton, former CEO of McKinsey says, "Many leaders benefit when they see the world through two lenses,

---

35 See Zaleznik, 1977.
36 According to https://www.vision2021.ae/en/uae-vision, H.H. Sheikh Mohammed bin Rashid Al Maktoum, vice-president and prime minister of the UAE and ruler of Dubai, launched the United Arab Emirates Vision 2021 at the closing of a cabinet meeting in 2010.

a telescope, to consider opportunities far into the future, and a microscope, to scrutinize challenges of the moment at intense magnification."[37] Consequently, crafting a vision requires a kind of bifocal competence of far-sightedness and near-sightedness.

John Kotter, organizational theorist, notes that most discussions about a vision tend to degenerate into the mystical, trailing down paths that leaders feel are beyond their grasp.[38] This adds to the characterization of a vision as amorphous and void of form. Kotter insists that, on the contrary, the job of creating a vision is neither magical nor whimsical but the tough, sometimes exhausting work of broad-based thinkers who are willing to imagine big and take risks. Certainly, intrinsic factors such as optimism, faith, possibility-thinking and spirituality are involved in the process of visioning, but in reality, a well-crafted vision sets boundaries on where the company is going and where it is not going. The boundaries of a vision must be clear enough to gain the conviction of action of employees.

Conducting business without a vision is wandering. Organizations that channel energy 'to their feet' rather than to the future may reap short-term gains with efficiency of task performance but have no idea about where they are headed. 'Going with the flow' is the state of mind. Vision brings intentional flow to how the company operates. Consider schools of fish. Even in ever-changing water, they move as one. That the course shifts often and quickly matters not. What matters is that they stay the course, moving in unison. A vision statement is a finely woven tapestry of organizational intent over the long term that has the strength of fiber to motivate employees and hold the enterprise together in the wake of unforeseen crises in the near term.

---

37 See Barton, Grant and Horn, 2012. Barton gave his famous lecture at Said Business School of Oxford University in 2015. One of the leadership traits he identified was the ability to think both long term and short term, which he likened to having both telescope and microscope.

38 Kotter, 1990.

Vision, Purpose, Mission: What is the Difference?

In addition to wanting to know *where* leadership is taking them, people also ask, *why* are we going there? *Who* are we? And *how* will we be traveling? Answers to these questions are found in purpose and mission. Purpose answers the reason for the company's existence. Mission is the engine and addresses how the company will accomplish its vision. Distinctions between the two can be confusing – and sometimes they are combined, which muddles things even more. However, to be successful, leaders must fully understand these critical aspects of a vision.

Purpose. Why are we going there? Why do we exist? What is the rationale? Why did we begin this journey in the first place? In the simplest terms, purpose is the company's objective. Clarity of company purpose is important because many employees cast their life's purpose on the company's purpose. Satisfaction with one's life's journey is connected to their own purpose, and this extends to the workplace. On a 2021 podcast hosted by Diane Brady, McKinsey & Company partners Naina Dhingra and Bill Schaninger presented research that indicated that during the COVID pandemic, nearly seven out of ten employees pondered their life's purpose. These were people who were frontline or customer-facing or critical workers. Those who reported that they live their purpose at work were six-and-a-half times more likely to report higher resilience. They were four times more likely to report better health, six times more likely to want to stay at the company, and one-and-a-half times more likely to go above and beyond to make their company successful. Other findings suggest that a good fit between personal and organizational purpose attracts talent.

Mission. Who are we? What is our identity? What do we believe in and stand for? How will we be traveling? What are the conditions under which we are going to grow the business? Answers to these questions explain the character of the company. The mission sets the boundaries of behavior to ensure that all stakeholders – from entry level to the board, to suppliers, to investors – operate with integrity. Executing the vision follows the canons of the mission. Organizational members face numerous ethical challenges during the course of work. Ethics vary from company to company and country to country. Knowing the company's values and ethics helps in the responsible management and resolution of these challenges, and in managing risks and shady or illegal behavior. In many ways, the mission establishes the standards of conduct and the expectation that organizational members will have the courage to honor those standards. Figure H shows the interrelatedness between purpose, vision and mission.

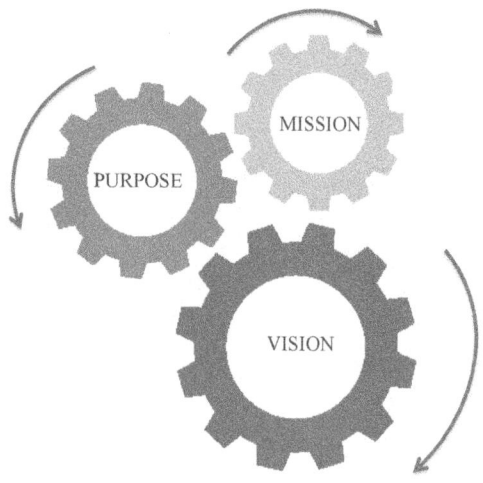

Figure H. Providing Direction with Purpose, Vision and Mission

But the Vision is Non-negotiable

Organizations can tolerate variation on the purpose, and benefit from different perspectives on mission, but cannot operate deftly without a vision. There are principles that leaders can keep in mind when preparing a vision.

1. ***Value Reflection.*** Embracing reflection can be imposing for some leaders, especially those who are more action oriented. They believe contemplation is a waste of time. Creating space between the incessant periods of action lets leaders see emergent patterns and themes and the connections among them. One of the most effective antidotes to the onslaught of daily distractions is slowing down the brain. Being still for just a minute is a good place to start. Simple breathing and mindfulness exercises are always useful. We tell leaders to slow down so that they can truly speed up. The reward is informed action.

2. ***Reflect on Multiple Realities, Antitheses and Paradoxes.*** What should be considered in a vision? Thinking holistically requires the leader's broadest and deepest consideration. Leaders who embrace multiple realities, antitheses, paradoxes and dilemmas tend to outperform their competitors. Take for example studies of the Toyota Motor Corporation[39] which found that paradoxes were an ingrained part of the culture at the car maker (for example, desiring stability whilst also desiring change). A classic business paradox involves people and profits. Even though experiences of paradox are not always positive, research tells us that embracing paradox reshuffles our deepest beliefs, providing alternative ways of looking at things. Moreover, contradictions and paradoxes must be regarded as on-going dilemmas to be managed rather than solvable problems that have a clear solution.

3. ***Deliver a Holistic Experience.*** For sure, a good vision reads well but it is more than a collection of well-crafted words. There is a feel about a good vision that evokes pride and a 'can-do' attitude among those inside the organization. The impact follows outside, attracting investors, customers, partners and future employees. A vision is the leader's projection, a best guess, of what the company should look like. This is

---

[39] Takeuchi, Osono and Shimizu, 2008.

determined after the leader does a thorough scanning of self and the world around them, involving others in the process. To gain followership, the final product must deliver a holistic experience, be acceptable to its audience and tap interest on multiple levels:

- On the *feeling* level, impacting the senses in words and message

- On a *perceptual* level, being inclusive of multiple perspectives

- On a *cognitive* level, offering a clear rationale

- On a *behavioral* level, sending a message that everyone is needed to realize the vision.

4. **Provide Direction, but not too Much.** Having a vision brings focus; however, too much focus defeats the intent. The intent is to show the direction and paint a picture of what the business will look like upon arrival. Consider the words of Peter Block, organizational consultant, from his 2008 *T+D* Journal article 'Leadership and the small group': "One's Vision is not a road map but a compass". He explains that a map describes terrain while a compass tells us if we are headed north, south, east or west, while navigating the terrain. With a compass, with a good vision, direction is never in doubt.

5. **Create a Shared Vision.** Just as critical as a 'compelling' vision is a 'shared' vision where ownership is distributed across the enterprise. Leaders are challenged in balancing their personal aspirations with those of members of the organization. This is understandable. After all, they are the ones who ultimately will be held accountable. But as they seek to stay personally connected to their visions, they must be tuned to the need to cultivate followership. It is the constant tug of what the leader wants versus what the company and employees need. A classic illustration of a shared vision comes in the story of a US Congressional tour of NASA facilities in the 1960s. Upon observing a woman mopping the floor, one of the lawmakers

asked her what her job was. Without hesitation, she replied, "putting a man on the moon". It was obvious that the woman understood NASA's vision. But, just as noteworthy was that she knew her role in making it a reality. When the vision is embraced by everyone, ownership is communal.

6. ***Do not Forget the Past and the Present.*** Because visioning is synonymous with the future, the past and present can be shortchanged. Visioning is not limited to the future. Time must be considered more broadly. A well-informed sense of the company's history reveals patterns and tendencies that must not be repeated or others that remain relevant. Current reality is a barometer of what is possible.

7. ***Keep the Ultimate Goal in Mind, Including When You Hope to Cross the Finish Line.*** Visualizing what winning looks like is a critical part of finishing the journey. Studies in neuroscience show that when we literally picture ourselves achieving a goal, our brain starts to find ways to get us there. But the true magic of a vision comes when one crosses the finish line on time. Ironically, we have observed a deflated reaction once a long-held dream has come to fruition. Changing situations have come into play that leave employees and leaders feeling as if they have fallen short. Because the trip to success is long, leaders forget their original intent. It is during these times that we take everyone back to the beginning. They realize that, indeed, they have been successful.

8. ***Update, but not too Often.*** One of the great myths about a vision is that it is long lasting and seldom requires review or updating. Because we live in a cycle of forever change, timeframes are not as fixed as they were in the past. Some timeframes can be as short as three years or as long as ten years or even more, depending on the vision and organization. Our guidance is that a vision should be updated (a) as the vision evolves; (b) when the firm changes its focus; (c) as the firm's circumstances change (e.g., finances, high turnover in leadership); and (d) when significant changes occur in its

CHAPTER THREE

environment. Multiple changes over a short span of time create confusion and an eroded brand identity.

9. ***Leadership is the Drum Major.*** This puts leadership at the forefront of realizing the vision. Leaders are expected to be role models of the desired future. While imagined possibilities can energize people, so too can energy be zapped by incongruency between what is promised and day-to-day experience. Many in the organization wonder at the introduction of a new vision if things are going to be as different as they are projected to be – whether they can trust leadership to stay the course and not leave them with another unfulfilled promise. Gestalt practice teaches the benefits of completing what one starts, because the brain has limited capacity to contend with too much unfinished business. Failure to complete 'units of work' leaves employees psychologically depleted.

The Importance of Being Reflective

Figure I. Reflection: A Way to See Ourselves

Reflective Observation is the learning mode associated with Vision Mastery and a key component of learning leadership. This learning mode emphasizes appreciation and understanding of relationships between events and people. It is where leaders pause to gain perspective about themselves, the enterprise, and the people and world around them. They are encouraged to view topics from multiple perspectives and in different ways, in the service of clarifying their own position. Research shows that leaders who take time to step back from the rush of daily activities increase their ability to examine different streams of data and information.

Reflection is also a place where sparks of knowledge and insight emerge. We hear from leaders who describe moments where they finally get an answer that has been evading them or arrive at a point of better understanding the assumptions, feelings and thoughts of others. The space between the frames of doing seems to activate one's creative genes. Seeing different ways of approaching problems or utilizing existing solutions is common. There are a range of ways that reflection can occur at the personal level: in solitude, with others, in stillness, and while active. Reflection is a way to see ourselves (see Figure I). Resources to aid leaders in the midst of their busy lives can be as simple as taking a deep breath before the next meeting or pausing for one minute to re-center themselves. It does not have to be time-consuming. Walking in particular has proven to be supportive of reflection. In fact, many sports activities can be conducive to reflection – biking, swimming, jogging, skiing. Other tools involve journaling, mindfulness exercises and yoga. At the group and company level, reflection means convening others to take a look at the company. Such a process involves allowing sufficient time to listen to, appreciate and build upon individual experiences and observations.

Reflection is not just about looking back; it spans timeframes. Taking stock of present performance and imagining the future success of the company are involved. And learning must be an integral part of reflection. Identifying when the company performs best and worst is an indispensable learning. In the RSVP Model, Reflective Observation is a legitimate form of learning and approach to leading, regardless of the format. The point of reflection is to take time to reground and rebalance.

Vision Inquiry

Vision involves asking and answering a key set of questions that inform decisions about the aspirations of the company. We have identified key questions that are useful prompts in developing vision. The questions are as important as the answers. Most of these questions have been used in many organizations and proven to be effective. They serve as a strong benchmark for reflection, but a constantly changing environment and company performance may warrant additional questions that are unique to a particular business situation and different from the ones presented here. Inviting an inclusive pool of stakeholders to participate in dreaming and imagining the company's future benefits the visioning process. Lively engagement results from challenging assumptions and the iterative cycles of questions and answers. Revisiting and refreshing the questions is as vital as updating the answers.

Questions of Vision Mastery

1. Who is included in the creation of our vision?

2. What is our process for collective and continuous reflection on who we are, what we want and how we will get there?

3. Who are we? (Purpose)

    a. Who were we? (Past)

    b. Who are we now? (Present)

    c. Who will we be? (Future)

4. What do we want? (Vision)

    a. What will the company look like in five years, in two years and a year from now?

    b. Who are the members of the company? Where do they

reside (top, middle, bottom)? How are we connecting and looking out for each other?

c. How are we operating?

5. How do we get there while living our values? (Mission)

a. How do we manage the tensions between people, profits and planet?

b. What do we stand for? What are the non-negotiables that represent our values and ethics?

c. What truly matters to us as a company?

d. Who truly matters to us as a company?

6. How do we monitor our progress?

a. How are we monitoring ourselves internally?

b. How are we monitoring the external environment?

c. How often are we revisiting our vision?

Skills of Vision Mastery

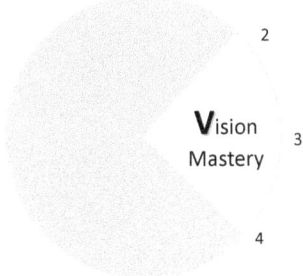

Reflective Observation is the mode of learning for Vision Mastery. It sits in the eastern quadrant consisting of Information Skills:

Creating at two o'clock, Gathering Information at three o'clock, and Analyzing Information at four o'clock (Table 5). Each clock position consists of three items.

Table 5. Vision Mastery

Learning Mode: Reflective Observation

Quadrant: Information Skills

Two o'clock: Creating

02:00 Imagining the ideal future

02:20 Managing multiple realities, dilemmas and differences

02:40 Exercising patience

Three o'clock: Gathering Information

03:00 Clarifying purpose, mission and vision

03:20 Assessing company climate and culture

04:40 Monitoring the industry and broader external environment

Four o'clock: Analyzing Information

04:00 Recognizing industry trends and patterns

04:20 Understanding implications of the changing environment

04:40 Synthesizing data into practical information and reports

Two o'clock: Adapting

2:00 Imagining the Ideal Future

Curiosity may have killed the cat, but in the ANK, its absence will doom the leader. The RSVP leader is grounded in what is actually taking place, while constantly searching for what else is possible. Curiosity is the strong desire to know or learn something. It is the lifeblood of innovation. We consider curiosity a crucial leadership skill. Jeff Bezos, founder of the e-commerce company Amazon, exemplifies the imaginative leader who is never satisfied with systems and processes that work. There is always a better way – we just have not thought of it yet. This functionally fanciful stance of dreaming what could be drives the eternal search for 'what else?' Animator and film producer Walt Disney embodied the ceaseless search for bringing the future into the present. At Disneyland, the amusement park he created, Disney went as far as to legitimize the science of dreaming with the job description of 'imaginer'. Imagination in a leader can also be a function of making unconventional connections or applying metaphors from different contexts to their work. For example, using a 'lateral arabesque' to describe moving employees who are not performing well to a different job with a longer title. Or a 'two-minute drill' to set a project pace. Holistic leaders draw on all their experience and all the possibilities to spark improvement.

2:20 Managing Multiple Realities, Dilemmas and Differences

Thinking differently about conflict is part of the RSVP leadership skill set. Difference fosters creation, the lifeblood of the growth that the organization seeks. *The difference that difference makes is creation.* Binary thinking ('either/or' thinking) reduces creativity. Thinking in terms of 'both/and' allows space for multiple realities to emerge. Viewing differences through the lens of multiple realities fosters appreciation and feeds cooperation. If an organization's commonality is its glue, then its differences are the spark of innovation. Former prime minister of the United Kingdom Winston Churchill said, "Show me two men who think exactly alike, and I'll show you one man I don't need". He recognized that difference is a prerequisite for creativity. But it is not a guarantee. What matters for leaders is to first ensure a diverse presence in all aspects of visioning and then provide a process for mining the richness that the diversity of thought provides. When the answer to a multiple-choice question is "all of the above", it is a dilemma. There is no way to eliminate the tension, but that tension can serve a creative purpose. The leadership skill in dealing with difference is responding with curiosity rather than defensiveness.

2:40 Exercising Patience

The fourteenth-century notion of patience as a virtue can easily get lost in today's need for instant gratification provided by technology. Patience is a virtue and a leadership skill. It is the capacity to accept or tolerate delay, trouble or suffering without getting thrown off course. Speed is a highly desirable asset (e.g., learning fast, detecting opportunity). So too is patience. It allows time for ample reflection, assimilation and deeper learning, and it mitigates impulsive action. Patience facilitates letting talent develop, ideas marinate and products find their niche. Remaining calm provides leaders with time to choose and respond logically, thus keeping them on top of the moment rather than being emotionally hijacked by it, especially in response to surprise, anger or disappointment. Warren Buffett, business icon and philanthropist, excels as a patient investor, not prone to the swings of reactive traders. Discerning when fast action or patience is called for is a crucial leadership skill. This is leadership wisdom. Entrepreneurs know the difference between *wasting* time and energy and *investing* time and energy. Patience is helpful in governance, ethics and providing perspective. It provides the ability to stay the course, a useful alternative to fast adoption.

Three o'clock: Gathering Information

3:00 Clarifying Purpose, Mission and Vision

Who are we? Why do we exist? Where are we going? And how will we get there? These are questions visionary leaders answer for those they lead. They see the whole situation, organize the experience of the team and offer a vision of the future. The leader's skill includes the ability to paint a vibrant picture and tell a compelling story which draws people in and inspires them to join in the pursuit of a shared purpose. Vision masters relentlessly observe and ruthlessly notice. Upon active reflection, they create multiple scenarios of a desirable future, choose one and share it. A vision is a disruption, shifting energy and outlining a new course. The leader need not be fearless, but they must be courageous. The moment a new vision is introduced, resistance shows itself in the form of fixation on the gap between where we are going, the vision, mission and where we are today. All insecurities are released. It requires courage to integrate all available information and shape it into a purpose and path, then invite others to follow or stay behind. This offer and response are the crux of leadership and followership.

3:20 Assessing Company Climate and Culture

The content and context of organizations are constantly changing. Rigorous monitoring of both provides up-to-date feedback to the leader on course correction measures. Organizational cultures are dynamic, living entities. The alignment of a company's culture with its values ebbs and flows, necessitating the leader's watchful eye. Data are the basis of informed change. Conducting culture assessments, using climate surveys, town halls, employee-engagement surveys, feedback tools and so forth, informs the reality of the current state. The RSVP leader utilizes this refreshed picture to discern when and what action is needed to redirect or reinforce the work environment. Holistic leaders realize that the map is not the territory. They combine the information that they have with their interpersonal skills to actively engage employees one-on-one, in teams or as a community, to get a feel for the nuances of employee satisfaction and the evolution of the company's culture.

3:40 Monitoring the External Environment

Attention and rigor are required of the leader when it comes to tracking ever-evolving industry and market conditions. Pleading ignorance is no excuse for the leader's oversight of environment trends impacting the organization. The decision to follow or buck current trends can only be made intelligently with data in hand. In the search-engine era, where the common expression for obtaining facts is "Google it" or "ChatGPT it", an enormous amount of information is accessible to everyone with tools. Systemically oriented leaders rely on professional and personal networks (trade shows, conferences, industry publications, consultants) to supplement and extend their intelligence about changing market conditions. For regulated businesses, this includes government and lobbyists as well. Leaders may also invest in building internal capability to anticipate and forecast embryonic patterns and trends in their operating environment. Successful entrepreneurs often see shifts and opportunities before anyone else. Vision masters do not wait to align with trends; they create the paths for others to follow.

Four o'clock: Analyzing Information

4:00 Evaluating Industry Trends and Patterns

Facts must be arranged into useful formats (themes, patterns and outliers). The leader as analyst and meaning maker invites others to join in participatory reflection to mine the richest, most diverse narratives about what is taking place in the environment and how best to respond to it. Pattern detection is an often-relied-on skill for the RSVP leader. It requires analytical versatility and robust consideration of all the data collected, looking through a variety of lenses and from diverse perspectives. Fresh eyes invited into the meaning-making process by the inclusive leader mitigate group think, fixed assumptions and 'blind spots'. They open the aperture for apprehending. Iconic American designer Ralph Lauren derives inspiration from relationships, landscapes, movies and life itself to tell the stories that shape his creations. His relentless vigilance and curiosity about what is happening all around, not just in his industry, position him to capture, create and lead industry trends.

4:20 Understanding Implications of the Changing Environment

Awareness of the changing context is a necessary but not sufficient position from which to lead. The potential impact of the change must be examined and understood. The learning leader is skilled at impact analysis – determining how the shifting context might force change in the organization's plans and strategies, estimating the extent of the effort required to adapt, and deciding how best to implement any changes. The ability to have systems in place in anticipation of changes in the external environment helps companies adapt more quickly. Insufficient lead time thwarts an optimal response. The iceberg watchers on the *Titanic* spotted the iceberg; they just saw it too late to allow the appropriate operational response. Over-reaction and under-reaction to emergent changes are equally bad. The skill of calibration is one arrow in the RSVP leader's quiver. Promptly noticing which way conditions are shifting, accurately assessing the threat posed by the shift, generating a tempered and well-targeted set of responses, confidently implementing the adaptation, and studiously tracking the internal and external impact of the actions serve the leader well when steering through change.

4:40 Synthesizing Data into Practical Information and Reports

We are now learning that the abundance of information is leaving us less clear about what is happening. It is not the amount of data on hand that adds value; it is the synthesis of it into meaningful, practical and usable formats. This is similar to the distinction between knowledge and wisdom: knowledge is knowing a tomato is a fruit; wisdom is knowing when not to use it in a fruit salad. The learning leader provides an interpretation of the analysis organized in a way which facilitates the transition from data to action. This interpretation can come in the form of reframing the analysis using a more accessible and digestible model. The SWOT (Strengths, Weaknesses, Opportunities, Threats) model is a classic example. It gathers and displays analyses as a holistic snapshot while framing categories which offer handles for action based on the differentiated

Table 6. The Vision Mastery Usage Indicator

Skill Area	Well-used	Under-used	Over-used
Two o'clock Creating	Taking time to reflect, dream and imagine the company's future; inviting others to contribute to the process; communicating and dialoging the purpose, mission and vision company-wide, using multiple media.	Not leveraging the power of slowing down to reflect; limiting participation and not allowing feedback in the process of creating the vision, purpose, and mission; lack of a strategic communications plan related to the vision, purpose and mission.	Failure to move beyond dream-state; excessive brainstorming and making too many changes, i.e., 'word-smithing'; too many inputs.
Three o'clock Gathering Information	Organized data gathering, e.g., employee, customer, investor, supplier satisfaction; company culture; diversity, equity and inclusion; industry trends; competitor analysis; timely updating of data and information.	Scope of data and information is narrow; using generalized data and information rather than inputs that are customized to the company and its needs; not using data and information.	Falling into data and information overload; using old data and information that is no longer applicable to current state.
Four o'clock Analyzing Information	Using the latest technology and analytics to determine state of the company and juxtaposing the findings against the current and anticipated state of the environment.	Not taking time to understand data and information and the implications for the future of the company; failure to map the various streams of data and information in order to see the biggest picture.	Getting stuck in analysis, i.e., 'analysis paralysis'.

categories (e.g., capitalize on strengths, mitigate weaknesses, seize opportunities and guard against threats). Reframing is a crucial skill for the RSVP leader as it shifts energy in the analytical process. One bank chief economist, frustrated by the CEO's negativity during the annual economic outlook briefing, reframed their presentation on "what could go wrong next year". The reframe shifted the CEO's stance to "it is not that bad".

Vision Mastery Usage Indicator

We have discussed how the Vision Mastery competencies are expressed and developed. Table 6 is a summary of the competencies when well-used, under-used and over-used.

Summary

Vision Mastery is a leadership-led process that lays out the company's future ambitions and serves as the foundation of strategic and operational priorities. A vision impacts the quality of relationships leadership forges with stakeholders inside and outside the organization. Though the primary responsibility for a vision falls to leadership, achievement relies on the buy-in of all members of the company who should be key players in the process. Full range of insight is needed in creating a vision. The work entails looking back to the past, assessing the present and projecting the future. Care must be taken that the vision serves as a compass that allows for contingencies rather than a detailed map full of constraints. Purpose and mission are often parts of a vision. A useful guide for distinguishing the three is to regard purpose as *why* the company exists, vision as *where* the company is headed, and mission as *how* the company will operate as it attempts to realize its vision.

Vision Mastery is the quadrant of the *Reflective Observation* Learning Style. On the Leadership Skills Profile (LSP), Vision includes the following sets of *Information Skills*:

CHAPTER THREE

- Creating (two o'clock)
- Gathering Information (three o'clock)
- Analyzing Information (four o'clock).

CHAPTER FOUR

Strategy Mastery

strat·e·gy / ˈstradəjē / from Greek στρατηγία stratēgia

noun

- a plan of action

- a general plan to achieve one or more long-term goals under conditions of uncertainty

- a plan to succeed against the competition often with limited resources

Rowing harder doesn't help if the boat is headed in the wrong direction.

Kenichi Ohmae, Management Theorist

Strategy Mastery is the ability of leadership to realize the vision by clarifying enterprise-wide priorities, allocating resources and defining processes for achieving those priorities. If today's companies are to remain viable, their leaders must build agile and innovative cultures that can make the strategic shifts required in an ever-changing environment. In this chapter, we recount the storied history of the rise and fall and rise again of strategy, greatly influenced by viewpoints from business and management author Henry Mintzberg.[40] *This is followed by general guidelines for preparing a strategic plan. We identify the skills and behaviors necessary for developing Strategy Mastery. The chapter concludes with a summary.*

Introduction

While all roads may lead to Rome, not all paths are worthwhile or profitable. Selecting the path most likely to realize the vision and purpose of the business is leadership placing its bets on success. Strategy identifies what works gets done, minimizing the probability of employees finding themselves at a crossroads, wondering if they should flip a coin to decide which road to take. When people do not know what to do, they do what they know. Conviction of action suffers in the absence of clear boundaries. We find it unfathomable that technology giant Netflix or Japanese retailer Uniqlo would operate without a strategy. A lack of strategic direction would be too costly for these companies. Time, money and other critical resources would be wasted in uncertainty and false starts. In the case of Uniqlo, surely the decision to concentrate on casual wear instead of luxury goods was an important strategic consideration. Because strategy focuses on *outcome* rather than *output*, it is more a leadership tool than a management tool. It is often said that strategy aims high – for example, to end poverty and not just to increase meals to hungry children; to be number one, not just to be among the top three; or to win the war, not just to win the battles.

Strategy is the calculation of survival in an environment of limited resources. It has been part of the natural make-up of civilization since humans decided to take action. Whether finding food or defeating enemies, people have always given consideration to how to meet their needs and ensure their safety. We see strategy most

---

40 To get a thorough account of Henry Mintzberg's perspectives on strategic planning, see 'The fall and rise of strategic planning of organizations' (Mintzberg, 1994). For an easy-to-follow chronological overview of strategic planning, see Pfeiffer, 1986.

apparently in the annals of warfare. In the fifth century BC, Chinese general Sun Tzu wrote his military treatise, *The Art of War*. To this day, this small volume of 13 chapters is an indispensable reference in military education worldwide. Strategy also is traced back to fourth-century BC Greek military history. In fact, the word 'strategy' is derived from the Greek word *strategos* meaning 'general of the army'. Strategos represented the various tribes of Greece and together they advised the ruling leader on the winning ways of war.

It is good to know that the ability to strategize is gender neutral. Take for example the sixteenth-century rivalry between the English Tudor queen, Elizabeth I, and her cousin, Mary Queen of Scots, that is legendary in depicting schemes of conquest. On this rivalry hung not just Mary's head but the religious affiliation of both monarchies. Unfortunately, Queen Mary lost her life and Queen Elizabeth went on to tally more strategic gains. Another example of strategy of historic proportions is found in the life and work of nineteenth-century abolitionist Harriet Tubman. Amid increased interest in Ms. Tubman, we are hearing more about her clandestine missions to free over 70 United States slaves using the Underground Railroad.[41]

According to Cynthia Montgomery, professor and former head of the Strategy Unit at Harvard Business School, in the role of strategist, the leader becomes the communicator of clear intent:

> It is the leader – the strategist as meaning maker – who must make the vital choices that determine a company's very identity, who says, "This is our purpose, not that. This is who we will be. This is why our customers and clients will prefer a world with us rather than without us." Others, inside and outside a company, will contribute in meaningful ways, but in the end, it is the leader who bears responsibility for

---

41 The Underground Railroad, led by US abolitionist Harriet Tubman, was a system of cooperation among active antislavery people in the US before 1863 by which fugitive slaves were secretly helped to reach the North or Canada.

the choices that are made and indeed for the fact that choices are made at all.[42]

With the clarity of direction that comes with a vision, leaders provide the platform to develop a strategy. The aim of strategy in the twenty-first century is to design a culture as an open system of coordinated effort that moves the vision closer to reality. Latitude should be wide at the functional and business-unit levels to allow for optimal internal integration and adaptation. This favors an emergent strategic process that sits both at the edges of the company, looking out, and at its core, looking in. A cadence of self-organization – of moving in and of moving out – is based on knowledge of the environment. Managers are given the latitude to reimagine products and services, how they might be produced and sold, and the capital and human resources needed. Old assumptions about developing strategy are supplanted by fresh models of organizing and operating that are driven by needs, capacity and capability.

The Rise of Strategic Planning

The seeds of strategy in business began to sprout at the turn of the twentieth century when planning became a core part of management theory. Worth noting are the seminal management perspectives of French mining engineer and CEO Henry Fayol. In addition to his principles of management,[43] Fayol identified six functions of management: forecasting, planning, organizing, commanding, coordinating and controlling. Planning, he explained, involves charting a suitable course of action, and he further asserted that planning is one of the fundamental truths for managing any organization.

Strategy made an important pivot in the early 1920s when the Harvard Business School developed the Harvard Policy Model, one of the first strategic planning methodologies for private businesses.

42 Montgomery, 2012, p. 2.
43 Published in 1916.

This systems approach helped firms align themselves with their environment through a detailed assessment of their strengths, weaknesses, opportunities and threats – otherwise known as a SWOT analysis. The major contribution of SWOT is its holistic simplicity in identifying factors that will affect future performance. With the help of SWOT, the objective of strategy became more than gaining advantage in battle or efficiency in production and administration. However, SWOT came with limitations. It did not describe how a strategic plan is developed beyond stating that a good strategy builds on strengths, takes advantage of opportunities, and overcomes or minimizes weaknesses and threats. It was obvious that strategy needed more. The Ansoff Matrix, a tool that helps leaders develop strategies by focusing on new and existing markets and products, moved strategy forward when it was introduced in 1957. With the Ansoff Matrix, risk assessment became an important strategic concern. About this time, strategic planning – the intricate process of developing a strategy – was becoming a common management tool as businesses of all size were attracted to an activity that held promise for directly improving the bottom line.

The Fall of Strategic Planning

Strategic planning reached its peak in the 1960s and 1970s but, by the 1980s and 1990s, it had become more of an exercise in producing a document – a plan – and less of a timely guide for collective effort. Strategic planning began to lose its glow. Four major issues converged to cause this shift:

1. Strategic plans were frozen in time
2. Participation was exclusive
3. Implementing the plan was not in the plan
4. Companies lost sight of the external environment.

Participation was Exclusive. Leadership is held accountable for strategy; however, this does not mean that strategic planning should be the exclusive purview of those at the top. At the onset of strategic planning, participation was a privilege, involving highest-level managers and leaders. Guidance of the process was given to a new breed of external consultant. Soon, a burgeoning industry of strategic planning advisors took shape.

In many ways, it made perfect sense that organizations entrusted such an essential decision-making responsibility to outsiders. First, strategic planning was a new frontier at the time. Second, part of the success of planning rested on mounds of data about the industry and, most importantly, about competitors. Businesses have always wanted to know how they compare and stack up against the 'opposing team'. However, during this era, access to data was not at the fingertips of leaders as it is today. Getting external assistance was wise. After all, taking the leap of faith to move from doing things the way they have always been done can be a difficult hurdle to overcome. An independent review by outsiders can be a strong catalyst for change. Not surprisingly, these points were not lost on strategic planners who came prepared to satisfy their clients' appetites to know if the grass were greener on the other side.

And the benefits did not end there. Consultants presented leaders with compelling narratives and colorful representations of a desired future at a time when organizations were placing great emphasis on looking ahead. Those who were new to this novel approach to strategic planning found themselves in the midst of a polished front-to-back production process. Many of them left meetings with consultants feeling part of an elite class of leadership – members of the strategic planning society. One downside of limited participation was that strategic plans offered exclusion in the face of broad impact which affected so many others in the organization.

Leaders have since learned that effective strategy benefits from many hands and minds. The greater the participation, the greater the buy-in. Management theorist Henry Mintzberg describes strategy as a process of synthesizing organizational learning, requiring broad membership to allow a ground swell of learning. In their highly effective Future Search writings and interventions, behavioral consultants Marvin Weisbord and Sandra Janoff advise leaders to "get the whole system in the room". Janoff so aptly asks, "If you are carving a direction without the whole system in the room, then who are you consulting?"[44]

Strategic Plans Were Frozen in Time. During the early days of strategic planning, there was an assumption that a plan would serve as a fixed guidepost for an extended period of time. Strategic planning sessions occurred in two- or three-year cycles, sometimes longer. This thinking resulted in plans fulfilling a range of purposes and finding homes in unexpected places. At best, they were codified pages of goals, objectives and detailed tactics. At worst, they joined the bookshelf collection of similarly celebrated but disposed versions of strategic plans from years before. Some plans contributed more to instant history than to future actions. Eventually, leaders began to realize that strategic plans must be constantly updated. Like the first time a vehicle is driven off an automobile lot, once a strategic plan leaves the pen or computer, some degree of value is lost.

The assumption of 'a plan forever' came at a time when the environment was relatively stable, but the context of business was changing. More and more, managers began complaining that strategic planning was impractical, far from the reality of their work. Leaders realized that one essential task of strategic planning is to keep data as current as possible. Creating a strategic planning cadence is useful for course correction.

Implementing the Strategic Plan was not in the Plan. Two-thirds of businesses fail to achieve strategic goals mainly because they do not have a system in place for executing the plan. Leaders who recognize the value of having a strategic plan and make the commitment to its execution consistently improve their company's performance. Such a commitment involves an additional plan, an **implementation plan**, that allocates resources (human, capital, financial, etc.) and maps the steps in the execution of the goals of the strategic plan.

[44] Sandra Janoff conversation, March 2021.

The message is that strategy is shaped by a series of fits and starts, and today's leaders must allow for course correction to adapt to a changing environment. Even though they hope to influence how their organizations will be affected, they cannot control the multiplicity of forces that impact them. The reality of emerging dynamics must be accepted and acted upon.

The Rise Again of Strategic Planning

Even though no one event can be cited as most pivotal in the rise again in strategic planning, we point to a 1992 *Harvard Business Review* magazine article by Robert Kaplan and David Norton where the Balance Scorecard (BSC) was introduced. The BSC was a step in addressing the disconnect between the internal environment and the external environment. It is a framework to implement and manage strategy. The idea is to 'balance' the strategy process by focusing on both internal and external factors in four financial and non-financial categories:

1. Finances
2. Customers
3. Internal processes
4. Innovation and learning capacity.

The BSC assumes a dynamic relationship among the four categories – for example, changes in innovation and learning capacity influence internal processes that in turn affect customer satisfaction, which also impacts financial results.

What Does Strategy Involve?

It Is about 'This Moment in Time'. The Balanced Scorecard is one of many models and frameworks for shaping a strategy. We emphasize again that a company's strategy is anchored in a clearly articulated, well-understood and shared vision that segues into performance. Ideally, when the time comes to develop strategy, the vision is already in place. Like vision, strategy serves a direction-setting role. The distinction is that vision is broad and less structured while strategy helps leadership decide where effort is best deployed at 'this moment in time' in service of realizing the vision.

Typically, a strategic plan consists of ends (*what* the desired outcomes are) and means (*how* the company will achieve the outcomes). The company's culture and resources – human, capital, financial – are among the internal considerations. Industry standing, consumer sentiment, technological change and government regulations are among the external forces.

While the language of a strategic plan is determined by the organization, **goals** are commonly used to describe the enterprise-wide priorities. In this instance, goals represent the desired outcomes. They are broad, yet specific enough that everyone understands them. Diving too far down with goals moves strategy away from leadership into management. Three-to-five goals aimed at clarifying the company's most immediate concerns are sufficient. Really, more than three goals sets the company on a path to creating a list. Sub-categories flow from each goal, such as *objectives*, followed by *tactics*, then specific *projects* that are assigned to project teams. The task of identifying these sub-categories of increasing granularity typically falls to managers and members of the key business and functional areas who have deep operational knowledge.

One method for organizing strategy is by cascading levels, for example, from *company* to *business* to *function*.

> *Company-level Strategy.* The overarching tier that runs across the company, the company strategy serves an integrating function.
>
> *Business-level Strategy.* The second tier, which flows from and links to the company-level strategy. Business-level strategy serves a differentiating role that allows

business-level leaders to customize their strategies and goals based on knowledge of their business while keeping in mind the overarching goals.

Functional-level Strategy. Still more differentiation is at play at the functional level that is formulated from the business-level strategy. Alignment and operational specificity are the aims at the functional level.

In this structure, the primary task at higher levels is integration, whereas at lower levels the task is differentiation. The process is a combination of flowing-up, flowing-down and flowing-across within each level.

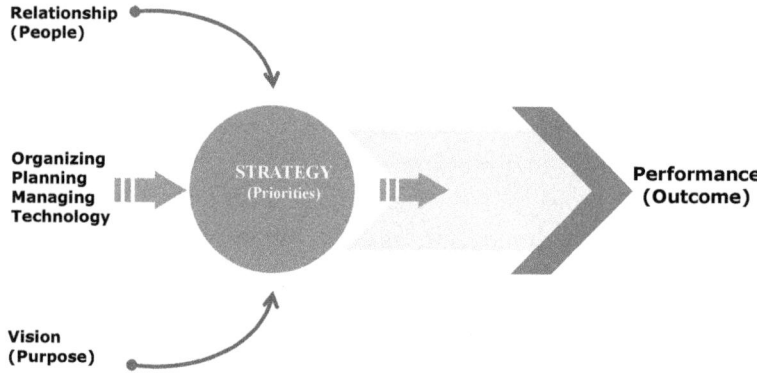

Figure J. Strategy Mastery: Linking People, Purpose and Priorities to Outcome

It Is 'Right-handed and Left-handed'. While strategizing involves separating what is critical now from what will be critical later, Mintzberg argues that shaping strategy is also about *synthesis*. It combines rationality and structure as well as intuition and creativity. The outcome is an integrated perspective on priorities that is neither too precise nor too ambiguous about what to do. Mintzberg says that, ideally, two kinds of people are needed in the strategy function: individuals who are right-*handed planners* and those who are *left-handed planners*.

- *The Right-handed Planner.* This type of strategist is organized – an analytic thinker who resembles conventional images of a planner. They create order, communicate clearly, conduct research, carry out analytic studies and monitor implementation of strategic goals. They keep detailed records and make full use of technology in the planning process. Their stance is driven by facts and can feel distant and impersonal, but they bring with them the assurance of accuracy.

- *The Left-handed Planner.* The other strategist is less conventional but can be found in many organizations. This planner is what Mintzberg calls a 'soft analyst', a creative thinker who seeks to open up the strategy process. The soft analyst is very pragmatic, conducting more 'quick and dirty' studies to encourage and inspire others to think strategically. This person is somewhat more inclined toward the intuitive processes identified with the brain's right hemisphere.

Many organizations need both types of strategizing. And it is top management's job to ensure that both approaches are utilized in the appropriate proportions. Organizations need people to bring order to the messy world of management as well as challenge the conventions that managers and especially their organizations develop.

Strategy Inquiry

Strategy involves asking and answering a key set of questions that inform decisions which determine the current priorities that will move the vision closer to reality. We have identified key questions that are useful in developing strategy. The questions are as important as the answers since they define the set of considerations used in formulating strategy. Most of the questions are associated with steps that have been used in many organizations and proven to be effective. These questions serve as a strong benchmark for making decisions about enterprise-wide priorities, but a constantly changing environment and company performance may warrant additional questions that are unique to a particular business situation and different from the ones presented here. An inclusive pool of perspectives – new and enduring – contributes to the ability of the company to truly embrace emergence. An assembly of varied stakeholders adds value through the questions they ask, the assumptions they challenge as well as the answers they provide. Refreshing the questions throughout the strategic planning process is as vital as updating the answers.

Questions of Strategy Inquiry

1. Who are we? (Purpose, Mission, Values, Ethics)

2. What do we want? (Vision)

3. Where are we now? (Current state: culture audit, market analysis, competitor analysis, strengths, weaknesses, opportunities, threats [SWOT] analysis)

4. How will we get there? (Goals)

    a. Objectives

    b. Tactics

5. What are our resources? (Financial and non-financial)

6. What is our plan for getting there? (Implementation plan)

7. Who will get us there? (Project teams)

8. How will we know when we get there? (Key performance and success indicators)

9. How do we monitor progress? (Dashboard)

10. How will we stay there? (Reinforce or Change Company Culture)

Strategic Agility

In the ANK, we advocate Strategic Agility, where strategic plans are more living documents and 'leading in a learning way' is the mantra. Continuous review, learning and adaptation are needed to stay competitive. Holistic approaches are employed that incorporate both left-handed strategies and right-handed strategies of the Mintzberg flavor. The process is more inclusive of stakeholders across the organization and across the external stakeholder ecosystem using Large Group Interventions such as Future Search, Real-time Strategic Change and Appreciative Inquiry. Adaptive processes, technology and artificial intelligence all contribute to more efficient and effective strategy. Many organizations do a routine strategy check at all leadership levels including the board level and in-depth reviews are conducted on at least a quarterly basis.

The Skills of Strategy Mastery

Strategy Mastery is related to the Abstract Conceptualization mode of learning and the southern quadrant of Analytical Skills: Organizing at five o'clock, Planning at six o'clock and Managing Technology at seven o'clock (Table 7). Each clock position consists of three items.

Table 7. Strategy Mastery

    Learning Mode: Abstract Conceptualization

    Quadrant: Analytical Skills

Five o'clock: Organizing

    05:00 Applying theories for data analysis

    05:20 Utilizing statistical tools and models

    05:40 Designing operational scenarios and simulations

Six o'clock: Planning

    06:00 Forecasting the future

    06:20 Creating a vision-based strategy

    06:40 Aligning goals to strategy

Seven o'clock: Managing Technology

    07:00 Utilizing current technology

    07:20 Managing privacy and cyber-security risks

    07:40 Ensuring accounting controls and financial resiliency

Five o'clock: Organizing

5:00 Applying Theories for Data Analysis

Donald Wolfe, a Case Western Reserve University professor, was known for his advice to students, "Data are just data until you translate them into information".[45] This is the essence of the leader as meaning maker. How are data informing you? The key to meaning-making is theories either created by the leader or retrieved from

---

45 Dr. Don Wolfe, Professor of Organizational Behavior, office conversation *circa* 1987.

existing studies. This suggest that leaders keep themselves apprised of the latest research and publications on leadership, management, and organizational behavior and change. Tapping resources that are both practical and grounded in current research is helpful. We are in the age of big data and leaders understand the implications of the information. Formulating practical theory is essential. Organizational theorist Kurt Lewin famously advised that "There is nothing so practical as a good theory". Analytics software can support the leader's own analytical capabilities, but part of the role of the leader is to translate and integrate these approaches to their organization's unique situation. The first step is appreciating the role a good theory plays in the strategy process.

5:20 Utilizing Statistical Tools and Models

Thorough data analysis, especially in this era of big data, can be a complex and overwhelming process. The learning leader can augment their analytical capability with models that relate to future demand for services and products, and with tools such as artificial intelligence (AI). Utilization models have limitations in that many assume that every situation is the same. Still, there are change models that factor a wide range of variables. Since all models have their flaws, the learning leader must understand the big drivers behind each model to determine where to tweak it if necessary. This model is sophisticated and applies probabilities to the various assumptions of modeling. Artificial intelligence is a powerful tool which demands more collaboration among people skilled in data management, data analytics, information technology (IT) infrastructure and systems development. RSVP leaders must ensure traditional organization silos do not hinder advanced analytical efforts, and they must support the training required to build skills across their workforces. Artificial intelligence also requires greater focus on risk management and ethics.

5:40 Designing Operational Scenarios and Simulations

Utilizing operational scenarios and simulations is an extremely useful way to engage leaders. It is an opportunity to explore the future of the company in the 'here and now'. This relatively instant feedback provides the learning leader with a chance to consider, weigh and retest a variety of alternative potential outcomes. One healthcare organization saw the results of 1,000 simulations of having a range of additional beds during the COVID pandemic. It was a powerful mechanism for building consensus on the target number of beds that were needed. Utilizing such tools requires someone with the expertise to lead the many back-and-forth discussions about parameters and assumptions, and to translate the findings into everyday language. This skill takes the form of storytelling, which is, itself, an invaluable tool for bringing people along. Without this ability, much of the power of the modeling is lost.

Six o'clock: Planning

6:00 Forecasting the Future

In the ANK, it is difficult enough to track accurately what is happening in the moment. The data may be available, but the meaning is not instantly recognizable. Forecasting the future is even more challenging. Some would say that forecasts should be dispensed with and simulations used instead. When correctly used, however, both forecasts and simulations serve a purpose in strategy, helping leadership understand a range of possible eventualities. Forecasts are predictions based on past and present data. The challenge with forecasting is that while past and current forces shaping the future may be known, the impact of these forces is hypothetical. Yet as imprecise as the forecasting process may be, it serves a useful purpose. It allows leadership to share their assumptions about the future. The forecast itself can help inform critical decisions on how to allocate resources and set overhead levels. Forecasts of the future are constantly refreshed when new data emerges. Leaders need to be proficient in using forecasting tools and explicit about the operating assumptions they are making in determining the direction of future trends. They also have to be aware of their biases, as these can distort the validity of the forecast.

6:20 Creating a Vision-based Strategy

Deciding how goals will be achieved resides within the leader's domain. The choices and paths selected and rejected guide the organization's work effort. Strategy bridges the vision and the operational work plan. This leadership skill is one of translation: converting the stuff of inspiration to a roadmap for action. The strategy offered has to connect to the emotional pull of the vision as well as to the practical need followers have to discern how the vision plays out in their role. Strategy answers the question "Why am I doing this work?" The leader establishes focus, definitively states what is in and out of bounds on the path to goal attainment. The world changes as it goes, so 'strategic agility' is required. The strategy will need to be adapted with built-in processes and checkpoints to ensure it leads rather than lags. Learning leaders involve their teams in the constant reviewing and refreshing of the strategy as conditions evolve. This is the essence of an 'agile culture' – one that is driven by knowledgeable, effective and efficient teams that operate with clear goals, roles, structures and processes, and interact in a combined internal and external ecosystem both physically and virtually.

6:40 Aligning Goals to Strategy

Strategy reflects decisions made that define how the vision will be reached. It is a process in prioritization. Aligning goals is where organizational capacity meets strategic ambitions. Leaders contract with their members in an interactive process and agree upon the goals, measures and projects that will realize the strategy. It is the responsibility of the leader to ensure that the agreed-upon goals are commonly understood and will, in fact, result in the implementation of the strategy. As a corollary, the leader makes certain that the metrics for goal attainment are aligned with desired behavior. Metrics shape behavior: people do what they are rewarded for and, at times, without regard for broader impact. The media are replete with stories of leaders focusing on personal goals at the expense of their company's credibility. Additional measures are required to balance things out. For example, leaders must take care that they are not asking the same parts of the organization to deliver on so many strategic goals that they get some progress across the enterprise but with thin results. Prioritizing is a leadership skill, and strategy is as much about saying what the organization will *not* do as what it will do.

Seven o'clock: Managing Technology

7:00 Utilizing Current Technology

The integrated nature of work today and the high reliance on technology demand leaders who can make technology-driven strategic shifts. Leaders must stay abreast of technology and digital trends and stay informed about how they benefit their organization. Searching for a technology solution is a smart, early step in converting strategy to implementation. Learning leaders embrace practical curiosity, and consistently seek new methodologies that increase efficiency and effectiveness, reduce costs and are consumer driven. While leaders do not need to be computer scientists, learning leaders seek out the advice and expertise of those who are. Managing the dilemma of 'do-it-yourself or outsource' involves consideration of one's attraction *and* aversion to technology, modeling learning outside one's specialty area and determining best use of the leader's time. A similar dilemma that needs to be managed is the urge to adopt new technology early or wait until it is reliable enough to be introduced.

7:20 Managing Privacy and Cyber-security Risks

Customers, citizens and patients entrust their privacy and digital well-being to organizations with whom they share their personal information. The almost daily announcements of security breaches from credit-card companies, retailers, airlines, healthcare systems and government agencies underscore the need for leaders to preemptively and aggressively provide for safe and secure protection of data. This accountability includes compliance with legal requirements such as the General Data Protection Regulations 2016/679 (GDPR), a data-protection directive regulating the processing of personal data within the European Union. Leaders must also protect the privacy of their own organization's members in all its forms. Managing these risks consists primarily of the ethical use and distribution of data, reducing the risk of a privacy or cyber-security breach, and having strong disaster-recovery and business-continuity plans in place if breaches and violations occur. In today's world, leaders should assume they will have a breach at some point and be proactive in mapping response.

7:40 Ensuring Accounting Controls and Financial Resiliency

Leaders set a boundary that all resource requests have to have a positive impact on finances, customer care and/or increased productivity; in essence, a cost benefit analysis must be in place. Accounting control guidelines must stipulate the allocation of resources from year-to-year. Limits should be in place to guarantee that only appropriate staff can access budget information. A budget timeline needs to be developed and shared prior to the budget process so that users know when they can access the system. Regarding financial resiliency, executive management has to be sure that all people who have budgetary control have a true understanding of the company's financial position. Margin improvement initiatives are inclusive, ideally starting from the bottom up to get buy-in. The knowledgeable leader understands that broad cuts are rarely sustainable. Such approaches do not identify specific waste and

Table 8. The Strategy Mastery Usage Indicator

Skill Area	Well-used	Under-used	Over-used
Five o'clock Organizing	Asking: "Do we have sufficient data, understand the data and what it means for the business?" Stating: "We have enough information!"	No examination of data from different perspectives and understanding the current implications for the business.	Analysis paralysis; requesting multiple analyses of the same data.
Six o'clock Planning	Flows from the vision; enterprise-wide representation; metrics and plan of execution; continuous monitoring of plan; strategies for emerging changes in industry and environment.	No planning; long planning intervals; lack of metrics; no execution plan; no monitoring.	Changing plans and goals too often; multiple plans at multiple levels.
Seven o'clock Managing Technology	Enlisting people closest to technology and stakeholders; utilizing technology tailored to company needs; consistent connectivity across the company and globe; provides tips for healthy use of technology.	Failures to use current technology; lack of integration of technology systems; failure to train employees in use of technology; little appreciation of the competitive advantage of technology.	Constant change in operational functions, additional training, worker stress, cognitive overload, confusion and possible addition; lack of coordinated effort, reduced interpersonal communication, and harm to the environment.

can lead to good performers being punished while poor performers remain under cover. Instead, time should be taken to identify waste and then eliminate it through processes such as re-engineering, which typically delivers outcomes that are more workable.

Strategy Mastery Usage Indicator

We have discussed how the Strategy Mastery skills are expressed and developed. Table 8 is a summary of the skills when well-used, under-used and over-used.

Summary

Strategy is a leadership function that flows directly from the company's vision. Strategizing as a practice has a long history. Examples of strategizing are found in ancient Greek and Chinese military operations, between warring cousins in England and Scotland, and in the courageous efforts of a US abolitionist. Planning became central to the rise of management theory at the turn of the twentieth century and, later, was greatly influenced by the Harvard Policy Model, one of the first strategic planning methodologies. Strategy hit its stride through the 1980s but suffered a downturn when (1) it became an exclusive process between the top tier of the organization and elite external consultants, (2) plans were never executed and (3) plans were misaligned with the reality of internal operations and the changing environment. Coming to the rescue was counsel from management theorist, Henry Mintzberg, and other theorists and practitioners that leaders should allow for emergent change in their deliberate or more fixed strategies. Today, strategy works best in adaptive and innovative cultures that stay attuned to the external environment. Essentials of strategy include a well-articulated and compelling vision, broad stakeholder and functional representation in developing strategy, performance indicators, and implementation plans and tools for monitoring and measuring progress.

CHAPTER FOUR

Strategy Mastery is the quadrant of the *Abstract Conceptualization* Learning Style. On the Leadership Skills Profile (LSP), Strategy includes the following sets of *Analytical Skills*:

- Organizing (five o'clock)
- Planning (six o'clock)
- Managing Technology (seven o'clock).

CHAPTER FIVE

Performance Mastery

per·for·mance / pər'fôrməns

noun

- the action or process of carrying out or accomplishing an action, task or function
- the actual output or results of an organization as measured against its intended outputs
- an act of staging or presenting a play, concert or other form of entertainment

> It is not the strongest of the species that survives, it is the one that is most adaptable to change.
>
> Charles Darwin, evolutionary biologist[46]

Performance Mastery becomes the watershed position on the RSVP Model, where it joins Relationship Mastery, Vision Mastery and Strategy Mastery to complete the cycle of 'what' leaders do. In this

---

[46] Michael Swinberg uses Darwin's comments as part of his discussion on how leaders can assist their team's resilience and adaptability. See https://drexel.edu/goodwin/professional-studies-blog/overview/2019/September/4-ways-to-boost-your-adaptability-skills

chapter, we expand the scope of 'return on investment'[47] beyond shareholders to include all stakeholders. We distinguish performance at the level of leadership from employee, operational and financial performance but emphasize that leaders must have knowledge of, and exercise appropriate oversight at these three levels. The Ten Leadership Mindsets of Performance and suggestions for ensuring enduring performance are identified to help leaders respond to the complex character of performance. The learning skills and behaviors necessary for developing Performance Mastery are included. This chapter concludes with a summary.

Introduction

Thus far, we have presented chapters on three of the fundamentals of the RSVP Model: Relationship Mastery, Strategy Mastery and Vision Mastery. Performance Mastery brings us full circle in our discussion of *what* leaders do. Presence Mastery, or *how* leaders do their work, follows in the next chapter. Because the RSVP Model is a revisioning of leadership, we had to ground ourselves fully in our approach to each component of the model. This was especially true for performance. Getting our arms around performance was not so easy because of the many connotations associated with performance, both in life and in the workplace.

The Experience of Performance

The need to perform is essential to human existence, whether surviving (feeding family, defending against natural threats, competing for scarce resources) or thriving (improving quality of life, extending community, sharing with others). Both require executing in new and better ways. In the workplace, performance is the ability of leaders to maintain the organization's existence

---

47 Return on investment, or ROI, is a mathematical formula that allows investors to compare the performance of a particular investment against that of other investments.

(surviving) and to create value and establish competitive advantage (thriving). Exceptional performance moves the world forward and leaves people and things transformed. Consider something as basic as a good performing car. It eases the worry of travel. Or, alternatively, the performance of a concert by cellist Yo-Yo Ma that will take our sensibilities to higher places. Performance brings with it the excitement of our favorite team making the winning score in a championship game. It is what we hope for our child in their first school play. Here, the perfect performance is just getting them to walk on stage, because remembering their lines is secondary. And at work, nothing compares to finishing a tooth-grinding project that did not reveal a positive outcome until the last second. The yells of "We did it!" demonstrate how a good performance stokes our emotions, activates our endorphins and inspires us to greater heights.

Performance and Leadership

As the study and practice of leadership has advanced on numerous fronts in the twenty-first century, perspectives on performance remain sadly stuck in the past. While the touch of leadership is wide, performance remains narrowly defined by bottom-line results and maximizing shareholder value. But this does not reflect today's reality. Leaders are ultimately responsible for overall company performance and accomplish their work with the help of a variety of constituents who deserve recognition for their contributions. As the face of a company, leaders recruit investors and also appeal to employees, customers and other stakeholders to follow them, often into uncharted waters. In the RSVP Model, performance is the leader's ability to recognize and return value to *all* stakeholders. This means balancing return on investment with such duties as ensuring job creation, fair wages, ethical practices, inclusive cultures, and a commitment to the organization's broader communities and the environment.

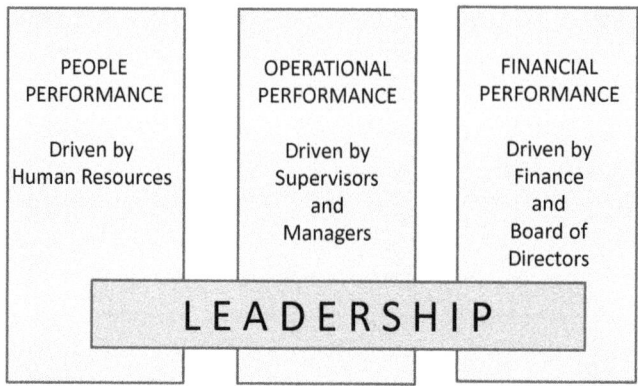

Figure K. The Three Levels of Performance

The Three Levels of Performance

Performance is leadership facilitating the realization of potential. It is the skilled enactment of leveraging relationships, achieving the vision and operationalizing the strategy. Leaders who replicate this process elevate themselves, their people, their companies and their communities. To do so, they must have knowledge of, and interface with performance at three key levels:

- *The People Level (Human Resources).* Employee performance is best supported by a sound performance-management system. Performance goals that are tied to company goals and objectives must be established for every employee. Fair and equitable rewards and recognition systems need to be established. Employee strengths and development needs must be determined, and a process for on-going monitoring, feedback and training must be created. Human Resources professionals, people managers and operational managers drive People Performance.

- *The Operational Level (Management).* Supervisors and managers aim for efficient operations with as few errors and quality issues as possible. Employing a skilled workforce, developing innovative ways of working, using the latest technology and equipment, prioritizing employee safety and well-being, complying with regulatory mandates and protecting the environment are part of performance at this level. Guidelines such as plan, execute, monitor and evaluate are often included. Managers and supervisors drive Operational Performance.

- *The Financial Level (Finance and the Board).* Performance at the financial level focuses on the financial health of the company, its bottom-line results and return on investor value. Success lies in the ability to generate income and manage expenses. Good financial systems such as a dashboard of key performance indicators (KPIs) and board oversight keep leaders on track while also following ethical and legal guidelines. Finance professionals and the board of directors drive Financial Performance (see Figure K. Three Levels of Performance).

Learning	Adaptation	Systems, Processes and Procedures	Experimentation	Continuous Improvement
Multiple Payoff Interventions	Feedback	Resistance	Delivering Results	Slowing Down to Speed Up

Figure L. The Ten Mindsets of Performance Mastery

The Ten Mindsets of Performance

Performance is a multilayered construct with many interpretations. This makes it difficult to consider performance in simple terms. Examining their personal mindset helps leaders understand their disposition toward performance. Mindset represents the totality of assumptions, beliefs and thoughts an individual maintains about a situation or thing. For example, a growth mindset consists of one set of assumptions, beliefs and thoughts, while a maintenance mindset is shaped by a different set. For a growth mindset, it is a case of "We can reach higher". With a maintenance mindset, the attitude is "We are at our best now". The difference is important because mindset influences behavior. The RSVP leader appreciates that a true performance mindset is an amalgamation of many, sometimes contradictory, factors.

1. ***Performance is Learning.*** Continuous learning sustains performance over the long term. A core part of the leader's role is to manage the dilemma between learning and performance (See Chapter One, Section C: Understanding Leadership). While knowledge is necessary for performing, learning is necessary for performing better. Every instance of performance is a learning moment. Unfortunately, when the pressure is on, there is a great temptation to forgo learning in the interest of performing. We see this when equipment maintenance is delayed so that the production line can continue running. The dichotomy between performing and learning is false because both must be done. One energy-sector chief operating officer illustrated how to hold both performing and learning when interviewing a candidate for her organization. She said, "Don't just tell me what you've done. Tell me what you've learned". A useful approach is to shift from learning in hindsight to learning in the moment.

2. ***Performance is Adaptation.*** In an environment that shows no signs of imminent stability, leaders must build their organizations not only with the capacity for continuous learning but

also for harvesting that learning with strategies for adaptation. Just as the human body readily adjusts to changing environmental circumstances, organizations must do the same. The difference is that adaptation is a natural process for humans but requires conscious effort in organizations. Without the ability to monitor, understand and respond to change, performance suffers, leaving companies at risk of extinction. This means building a culture where quick responses are a routine part of everyday life. Furthermore, anticipating change is just as much a part of adaptation as reacting to change. Leaders are advised to devise strategies to track trends and patterns to help foretell potential shifts in the environment.

3. *Performance is Systems, Processes and Procedures.*[48] To deliver results, an operational pathway must be in place that connects people and the work they do. Such a pathway relies upon efficient and effective systems. A system is the general set of interdependent and coordinated activities that make it possible for an organization to deliver products and services in a timely and seamless manner. When a customer complaint is escalated to a supervisor and not addressed at the first point of contact, the system is a hindrance to, and not a helper of, performance. A good Human Resources system is one that not only tracks recruitment, retention and departures; it inquires into the experience of acceptance and belonging of current and departing employees.

Systems consist of processes and procedures. A process is a *detailed map of sequential activities or tasks* that meet a specific need for a specific role or purpose. Procedures are the *protocols and guidelines* that clearly outline the steps involved in a process. The airline industry is the benchmark of efficient and effective systems. Those who are responsible for air travel around the world follow similar protocols. Regardless

---

[48] Insights retrieved 4 June 2022 from: https://www.pcg-services.com/is-it-a-process-or-a-procedure-understanding-the-difference.

of air carrier, their pilots and flight attendants know what to do and say upon take-off and landing. And to safeguard proper protocol, flight attendants in training, and often those attendants with longer tenure, will read the procedures. Leaders in all industries must not ignore the importance of systems, processes and procedures in gaining competitive edge.

4. *Performance is Experimentation.* Active Experimentation is the mode of learning associated with Performance Mastery and the lifeblood of learning by doing. A healthy appetite for trying new things is needed to move from intent to execution and from model to action. The purpose of an experiment is to learn, to generate data that inform the possibility of performing at a higher level. When properly executed, experiments result in real-time adaptation. The power of the experiment lies in what is known as creating a 'safe emergency', which involves some level of risk combined with a degree of prudence. In an experiment, the leader becomes a test pilot. We have learned from history that some of the most prosperous societies – Ancient Athens, Renaissance Italy, nineteenth-century Britain – were oriented towards experimentation and risk-taking. In the true spirit of experimentation, the answer to the question "What will we learn?" is "I do not know", because the knowing is yet to be revealed. Most companies are familiar with experimental research, but experimentation also can be applied more broadly to day-to-day activities, for example, holding meetings later in the morning rather than at the start of the day, or having everyone sit in a different seat at each meeting, or having leaders committing to making contact with a person with whom they are unfamiliar in the company. One of the keys to a successful experiment is to convene groups and teams to learn quickly, collaboratively and collectively.

5. *Performance is Continuous Improvement.* Performance is always about improvement. The pursuit of better performance

has captivated leaders from all domains – non-governmental, small business, education, the arts, sports, military and empires. 'Kaizen', the Japanese word for continuous improvement, has been central to Japanese quality leadership for decades. Continuous improvement is not about brief sprints of aggressive energy in pursuit of shorter-term gains but rather the commitment to a lengthy, steady marathon towards the longer-term goal. It involves the leader guiding the journey from what is familiar to what is new and unprecedented. The availability of resources complicates the pursuit of continuous improvement. Many companies tap their 'cash cow' businesses – those producing predictable results and reliable returns to investors – to fund riskier, more innovative ventures. Selective use of 'close enough' is another strategic stance when resources are limited. But even those outcomes that are close enough warrant a minimal amount of oversight to determine if results are true improvements.

6. *Performance is Multiple Payoff Interventions.* The learning leader is a change catalyst, juggling multiple initiatives. Multiple payoff interventions (MPIs), which utilize a complex-systems principle of having more than one means to an end, are one way to optimize results. For instance, leaders can explore different strategies for a particular issue or attend to and compare a number of issues at the same time. Given the number and complexity of situations facing organizations, a linear problem-solving approach is impractical. A technology leader in our research commented that "There is always a scarcity of resources. Strong leaders look for ways to leverage existing resources, scale through automation and recurring mechanisms, and reduce non-value-added processes". Strategic ambition suggests integrated and parallel efforts rather than siloed and sequential ones. The holistic RSVP leader never does anything that only accomplishes one goal. One of our client organizations decided that three major business performance-improvement initiatives were necessary: shifting to a more collaborative culture, upgrading the level of leadership talent,

and providing diversity, equity and inclusion training. Instead of three separate work streams, they created one educational intervention for all leaders with the design driven by achieving the three goals. This MPI approach offered resource efficiency, synergy and an integrated learning experience.

7. *Performance is Feedback.* Feedback is an indispensable tool for improving the performance of a person, group or system. It must be timely, specific, consumable and, most of all, fact based. Judgment in feedback fuels defensiveness, while data drive adjustment. Both formal feedback (scheduled meetings) and informal feedback (during day-to-day interactions) are amenable to open discussion about what is working well and what can be improved. Not surprisingly, positive feedback is often undervalued. Negative comments get attention. Still, presenting the full range of data is advised. It removes guesswork. And it must be specific. Non-specific feedback even when positive is confusing. "Continue doing what you are doing" or "You must do better" are generic statements. "Keep including your staff in reports to the board" and "Distributing the agenda before meetings would be helpful" are specific. Moreover, feedback must point to the value of employees and how the work they do contributes to the success of the company. In a 2017 global survey, management-consulting firm McKinsey found that 54 percent of respondents said their performance reviews had no positive impact because there was no mention of the connection between the company's performance and their performance.

8. *Performance is Resistance.* Performance can be fraught with resistance because performance improvement means change. The quest to produce results is a call to action. It also breeds resistance. Leaders hope for universal support in pursuing better performance, but this is not the case. Change is often least wanted when it is most needed. And many times, the greatest challenge for a leader is their own resistance. Everyone wants to sign up for better performance, until they discover

the price of admission is the personal discomfort that comes with it. The litany of reasons for resistance is familiar:

- We know we need to change, but now is not a good time. This is a high-risk situation. We will change when there is not so much at stake.

- Things are too unsettled right now. We will change when things calm down.

- We do not have enough data. After we collect more, we will know whether, when and how to change.

- We are beyond our capacity to absorb the degree of change we are currently experiencing. We have to wait until we adjust before we initiate more change.

All of these responses and reactions are valid and understandable sources of reluctance, and they must be acknowledged. They also point to the reality of the depletion of physical, emotional, psychological and spiritual energy among employees – referred to as 'change fatigue'. Employees are swamped by the unceasing tide of both discretionary and non-discretionary change. Leaders are not exempt from the heaviness of change and are overwhelmed too. Unfortunately, when forced to choose, they focus on the basic products, services and programs, often sacrificing or paying lip service to real change and innovation. And employees follow their lead.

9. *Performance is Delivering Results.* The purpose of performance is to get to the finish line; to complete the work that has started. This is very difficult to do when so many tasks are competing for so little time. It falls to leadership to ensure that the job gets done. Unfinished tasks rob individuals, groups and the organization of energy. Gestalt practitioners use a tool called a 'unit of work' (UoW). With a UoW, large, macro tasks are designed with smaller, medium and micro UoWs in mind. A UoW is a way to organize change

initiatives into manageable and coherent 'chunks of change'. Three overarching phases are involved: the Beginning, the Middle and the End (BME).

a. *Beginning.* Determine the work. (Collect data, determine findings.)

b. *Middle.* Do the work. (Mobilize energy, take action, make an impact.)

c. *End.* Close the work. (Evaluate, disengage, rest, move on.)

Each phase is further organized into sub-phases of a BME. This sub-categorization continues as long as it is useful to the work.

10. ***Performance is Slowing Down to Speed Up.*** Performing fast enables learning fast. Software companies get new code out as fast as possible at what some call the *minimally loveable level*, gather data and iterate. This is referred to as 'Fail Fast Forward'. But slowing down also contributes to performance. Paradoxically, slowing things down speeds things up. Let us remember that active reflection is action! Performing in the usual way translates into working on autopilot – habitually and, hopefully, effectively. But innovation is not included. Asking, "How might we do this differently?" invites pause and contemplation. Exceptional athletes describe themselves as seeing the game in slow motion. Decelerating the action is the primary transition challenge athletes face when performing at a higher level of competitiveness. Wayne Gretzky, considered the greatest ice-hockey player of all time, developed the ability to view the whole ice surface and slow the action down in a way that allowed him to see where the puck would be.

Ensuring Enduring Performance

Because *exceptional* performance over the long term is rare, we felt a need to share our thoughts about how companies can *extend* performance. Three things came to mind:

- Sustaining the positives – building on institutional knowledge and wisdom
- Fixing-up the foul-ups – rebounding and recovering
- Actualizing the possible – innovating.

Sustaining the Positives – Building on Institutional Knowledge and Wisdom. "If it ain't broke, don't fix it" is an old adage that suggests we should not try to change something that is working well. The expression was made popular in the late 1970s by Thomas Bertram Lance (Bert Lance),[49] director of management and budget in the administration of US President Jimmy Carter. Lance believed that the government could save billions of dollars by adopting the motto. In a 1977 issue of *Nation's Business*, Lance was quoted as saying, "That's the trouble with government. Fixing things that aren't broken and not fixing things that are broken". The suggestion is not to tinker with the things that work. Instead, concentrate on what is not working: either improve or eliminate them. However, today's relentless pace of change has forced leaders to consider an alternative expression, "If it ain't broke, *break it*". This means never being satisfied. Yet, there is logic in sustaining systems that are producing desired results.

Good leadership includes the ability to appreciate what is working well. We find this competence in successors who inherit high-performing organizations and have the foresight to lead by

---

[49] "However, while it seems that Lance popularized the term, he was not the first to use it. For example, The Phrase Finder points to a reference in the Texas newspaper, the *Big Spring Herald*, December 1976" (Retrieved 3 October 2022 from: https://www.bookbrowse.com/expressions/detail/index.cfm/expression_number/326/if-it-aint-broke-dont-fix-it).

building on strengths. They are not tempted to make false progress by changing simply for the sake of changing. Much of the time they do not receive the accolades bestowed on their predecessors, but they are important because they are 'sustainers'. Consider Tim Cook, who followed Steve Jobs at Apple, the multi-national technology company. Cook embraced what was working at Apple as a springboard to what could be better. Other sustainers include investor Warren Buffett, football club Manchester United and the Bolshoi Ballet dance theatre.

Our advice to successors is to value the wisdom that already exists in the company. Many family businesses that fail do so because the second generation misses this very practical aspect of performance. Notable exceptions are found at luxury auto maker Bayerische Motoren Werke, better known as BMW, and fragrance and skincare manufacturer Estée Lauder. The RSVP leader notices what is currently working and how it is working. They see what others miss due to familiarity. This awareness naturally evokes fresh perspectives on how to sustain and improve performance. Reinforcing what is working – catching people doing something right – paradoxically improves performance by sustaining with emphasis.

Fixing-up the Foul-ups – Rebounding and Recovering. Identifying opportunities to improve substandard results is a matter of discerning the gap between what is expected and what is currently being delivered. Leaders who are proficient in performance examine all angles of the RSVP Model to create hypotheses about what is not working as planned and what corrective action must be taken. Rigorous forensic exploration seeks to understand the variance between the promise and the practice. Many construction projects include a specific phase of the process to address discrepancies. It is known as the 'Fix-Up the Foul-Ups (FUFU) Phase' and its purpose is to correct errors made in converting blueprints to structures.

Looking at 'the glass half empty' is a useful orientation in performance improvement. 'Turn-around' specialists are well-versed in the science of problem detection and correction. Experience has taught them to distinguish between obvious remedies and situations that warrant out-of-the-box thinking. A recurring pattern we have observed among turn-around specialists is their reliance on a systems perspective. They do not accept the presenting problem at face value. Instead, they focus on the bigger picture and the relationships among the parts. For example, poor inventory management could be the presenting issue, but exploring the relationship between sales and manufacturing takes the issue from symptom to root cause.

A critical eye is necessary for uncovering performance-improvement opportunities. Learning leaders are inclusive and invite everyone involved with the work to participate in continuous improvement. They explicitly make correction as much a part of the work as execution. But caution must be taken to avoid the pitfall of assigning blame. Often, there is a need to find a culprit for foul-ups. But fingers should be pointed toward the correction opportunity. What matters is learning. A debrief – a form of deconstructing a previous event or experience, like tennis greats Serena and Venus Williams reviewing film of their games – generates learning for all, not just those involved in the action. The greater the value placed on collective learning, the more likely it is that results will improve.

Actualizing the Possible – Innovating. The examination of performance is not only about learning and adaptation but also about learning and innovation. It reinforces leadership as an innovation function. Learning leaders refuse to accept any level of performance, however impressive, as the best possibility. They relentlessly pursue something better. Success is the platform from which the drive to discover new opportunities begins. Acknowledging current success fuels innovation and challenges fixed mental models.

A possibility mindset quietens organizational doubt and infuses courage into the company. The courage to contest 'what was' and 'what is' puts sacred cows at risk.[50] 'What can be' becomes the

---

50 In business, a sacred cow is an outmoded mindset that inhibits change and prevents responsiveness to new opportunities.

guiding principle. It prompts persistence to improve even what appears to be perfect and beyond improvement. This is based on what psychologists refer to as the 'illusion of control', where humans feel a sense of agency over events that they cannot actually influence. City planners utilize this phenomenon when they design "placebo buttons" at pedestrian crossings. This practice serves leaders well when they encounter performance-improvement situations seemingly out of their control. Engineers are of a similar mind when they program the 'Close Door' elevator button. Most of the buttons have been nonresponsive to touch since the early 1990s to all but emergency responders! However, during the COVID pandemic, out of the necessity to limit the spread of the pandemic, elevator passengers were allowed to close the doors.

Performance Inquiry

Performance is what gets the work done in organizations. We have identified ten key questions that are useful in improving performance. Good questions seek exploration, not confirmation and are intended to evoke, not prescribe. They serve as a strong benchmark, but a constantly changing environment and company may warrant additional questions that are unique to a particular business situation where a more inclusive pool of perspectives would benefit the exploration. Value comes through the assumptions that are challenged, the questions that are posed, as well as the answers provided. Refreshing the questions throughout the inquiry process is as vital as updating the answers.

Questions of Performance Inquiry

1. What is working well about the way we currently perform? Why?

2. What suggestions for improving performance do those who actually carry out the work have to offer?

3. How can we apply fresh eyes to the situation?

4. What is the low-hanging fruit representing easy wins and traction early in the improvement effort?

5. What unspoken beliefs are we operating under? (Ask "what if?")

6. What are the underlying assumptions we are making about how performance is best delivered?

7. What assumptions and boundaries can we challenge to stimulate thinking?

8. What have we learned from our performance experience and results to date?

9. What experiments can we craft to test improvement opportunities?

10. What mechanisms (existing or newly created) foster quick and broad distribution of improvement learning?

Skills of Performance Mastery

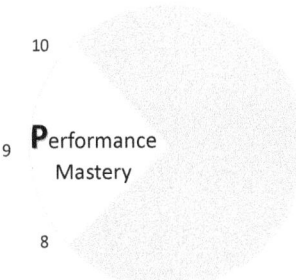

Performance Mastery is associated with the Active Experimentation mode of learning and the quadrant of Action Skills: Setting Standards at eight o'clock, Taking Action at nine o'clock and Innovating at ten o'clock (Table 9). Each clock position consists of three items.

CHAPTER FIVE

Table 9. Performance Mastery

Learning Style: Active Experimentation

Quadrant: Action Skills

Eight o'clock: Setting Standards

08:00 Committing to a diverse, equitable and inclusive workplace

08:20 Designing systems for employee well-being

08:40 Clarifying performance goals and metrics

Nine o'clock: Taking Action

09:00 Influencing and guiding others

09:20 Getting things done

09:40 Being decisive

Ten o'clock: Innovating

10:00 Being a catalyst for change

10:20 Capitalizing on opportunities; being entrepreneurial

10:40 Taking risks

Eight o'clock: Setting Standards

8:00 Committing to a Diverse, Equitable and Inclusive Workplace

Performance is influenced by employee and leader behavior, and by the workplace environment or culture. The culture is shaped by formal policies and informal norms and unwritten rules. It is the leader's role to ensure the standards of expected behavior in the workplace. Policies delineate and reinforce desirable, productive and ethical behavior. Leaders are subject to the same behavioral standards and are expected to manifest the values by living them out. Employees have the right to expect a working environment where everyone feels included, valued and encouraged to contribute to their fullest. They can also expect equal treatment (e.g., pay, training, opportunity, respectful behavior) regardless of their origin or identification. The rich tapestry of a diverse workforce contributes to a sense of belonging and promotes high performance. On gender or racial and ethnic diversity alone, McKinsey's latest research finds that companies in the top quartile on these dimensions are more likely to have financial returns above their national industry medians. Sensitivity, courage and the lens of multiple realities are qualities that enable leaders to maintain the integrity of an empowering culture, one that does the right thing for its people, its customers, its organization's success and its community.

8:20 Designing Systems for Employee Well-being

Leaders define, test and move boundaries that provide meaning (definition), establish limits and set expectations. Boundary-management skills are evident in the design and constant updating of structures and processes in organizations that set the limits of interaction. These systems institutionalize a leader's strategy for creating safety for employees; for motivating and rewarding them; and for generally helping them navigate their way toward contribution and belonging with purpose in the organization. Systems such as those for recruitment, talent development, compensation and benefits, and managing employee grievances lay the foundation for organization culture. The desired culture is the foundation for Human Resources (HR) systems. From enrollment to retirement, HR systems provide structural support to leaders in their quest to keep followers safe, focused, productive and on the payroll. They also enable leaders to replace workers who prove unsuitable for job requirements in a respectful manner.

8:40 Clarifying Performance Goals and Metrics

Leaders must create a sense of urgency. But if everything is urgent, nothing is. Performance goals and metrics create priority and a framework for accountability. Jointly setting performance goals establishes a contract between leader and follower about what matters most and how individual success will be monitored and measured. A clear set of metrics defines the scorecard that will be the basis for performance assessment. It is true that what gets measured is what gets attention. And it is also true, as Albert Einstein said, "Not everything that counts can be counted, and not everything that can be counted counts". The skillful leader discerns how the various aspects of an employee's contribution are to be weighted and valued for their contribution to the performance of the whole. Metrics provide the leader with data indicating where their intervention and mid-course correction are warranted. Leaders hold themselves accountable for actions and outcomes. They must also hold the people who work for them accountable. Lack of accountability in a team ultimately leads to decline and malaise. Robust accountability mechanisms reinforce self-responsibility and self-empowerment.

Nine o'clock: Taking Action

9:00 Influencing and Guiding Others

Orchestra conductors do not play an instrument. They lead by directing the performance of others. Similarly, leaders are skilled at orchestrating complex projects into manageable elements, distributing assignments to individuals and teams, directing the flow of work, monitoring performance, adjusting as necessary and creating a positive environment. Leaders know what and how much to delegate. Delegation is an act of trust and empowerment. The risk is not being in control. In fact, people can only control their own perceptions and behavior, but leaders are tempted to try to control others because they are accountable for results. Letting go of control is a leadership skill. Leaders develop team members, trust them to perform, provide clear direction, support them through feedback and hold them accountable. Leaders influence by shaping the work environment, keeping it from drifting into the negative, what the military calls 'energy suck'. Leaders model by sharing their own energy. This is more than leading by example: sharing energy is physics. The holistic leader celebrates victories big and small as a way to sustain positive energy.

9:20 Getting Things Done

In the words of a technology executive interviewed for our research study, "There are a lot of big thinkers/talkers out there. Big thinkers who can actually execute, iterate and deliver results separate themselves". Delivering results takes more than moving to action; it requires follow-through and driving to resolution. These leaders create processes that build a sense of urgency and excitement in their followers, through whom things are done. This urgency is the most positive and impactful force when trying to get jobs, missions and work accomplished and scaled. The skill set that gets things done includes creating clear assignments, following up, conducting gap analysis and providing the missing tools. Completing units of work (UoWs) and acknowledging their completion generates the energy that feeds into subsequent tasks.

9:40 Being Decisive

Leadership is situational. There are times when openness to the ideas of others is best, and then there are times when clear direction from the leader is needed. In times of crisis, when action is demanded, people look to leaders for their decisiveness. The skilled leader recognizes when a situation requires a quick response. Crisis-mode leadership warrants instinctive reaction rather than considered reflection. There is no time for the usually prized reflection. To quote one senior executive and former army leader, "It is easy to be indecisive. There is always more research, input or planning to be done and these things have value, but your team must know that a clock is ticking and that you have the character, will and courage to decide. Further, that you cherish action. That you have a sense of urgency that is greater than your desire for your own personal safety or reputation". The urgency of the moment compels the leader to scan, consider and decide with speed and agility.

Ten o'clock: Innovating

10:00 Being a Catalyst of Change

In chemistry, a catalyst is an outside agent added to increase the rate of a reaction. Leaders are change catalysts, responsible for igniting and accelerating organizational change. Change-agent skills for the holistic RSVP leader include the ability to scan the environment, calibrate readiness and leverage points, initiate disruption, recognize and channel resistance into a positive force, and strategically marshal resources in support of change and learning. The change leader interrogates the status quo. Calling underlying assumptions into question demands courage, as provoking power risks losing one's privilege. Long-term success necessitates that the leader does not become the kind of catalyst that is consumed in the process. The interrelated and complex nature of organizations rewards leaders who are able to use multiple payoff interventions (MPIs); who never do something that only achieves one goal; who, for example, design a process that combines leadership development, diversity and inclusion, and team building. This type of innovation requires systems thinking. As organizational transformation relies on leveraging synergy and trust, building trust recurs as a leadership skill. This is particularly true when leaders ask followers to join them in disruption and co-creating change.

10:20 Capitalizing on Opportunities; Being Entrepreneurial

The ability to notice, or even anticipate, the unexpected disruptive event and the ability to genuinely feel the possibility in the situation are two skills which give leaders an edge in maintaining or improving performance. Opportunity is an unplanned experiment. *Carpe diem* is an orientation of making the most of whatever presents itself. Learning leaders do not just substitute by rote the word 'opportunity' for 'challenge', they actually feel the fire in the reframe. It is not the word; it is their attitude that drives a search for capitalizing and innovating. Plato said, "Our need will be the real creator" or, as the English proverb restated it, "Necessity is the mother of invention".[51] Entrepreneurial leaders look for every opportunity to improve. They welcome the invitation to create. It is in this space that entrepreneurs move rather than moan. The opportunities provided by the COVID pandemic lockdown resulted in mass migration to working remotely, the development of corresponding technology, inestimable environmental savings, creative ways to meet customers' needs and accelerated trends like a cashless society. Leaders see the opportunity to move; great leaders see the opportunity earlier and respond faster.

10:40 Taking Risks

Risk management has a different meaning for leaders in the ANK. It is more about their personal risk taking in an environment where little is certain. Taking informed, considered risks is a must-have skill competency of innovation and performance improvement. In the Volatility, Uncertainty, Complexity, Ambiguity (VUCA) environment, there is little certainty and best practices are quickly outdated. Thinking it out relies on reflection and researching the past, which helps. Acting it out provides more information. The learning leader's skill portfolio also includes proficiency in Active Experimentation – learning by doing, an action orientation. Innovation and improvement are informed by researching the present. Try something, see what happens and what can be learned, then try something different. Discipline, spontaneity and discovery combine to feed real-time learning and point to new paths and

---

51 In the Socratic dialogue *Republic*, Plato famously wrote, "Our need will be the real creator", which was molded over time into the English proverb "Necessity is the mother of invention". Originally retrieved 26 October 2020 from a posting by Nicole Lotz in Design comment.

Table 10. The Performance Mastery Usage Indicator

Skill Area	Well-used	Under-used	Over-used
Eight o'clock Setting Standards	Provide structure, boundaries and clear expectations.	Confusion about goals and roles; wasted energy; homogeneous workforce that limits innovation; unsafe work environment.	Rigidity and bureaucracy; little room for experimentation; too much care and feeding of the system at expense of results.
Nine o'clock Taking Action	Execution with conviction; experimentation; efficient operations; ability to flex and adapt in real time.	Too much focus on process over results; lack of an over-arching work map that provides direction; floundering.	Non-stop action to the point of employee exhaustion; confusing activity with progress; applying same procedure to every task.
Ten o'clock Innovating	Institutionalizing systems that support and reward innovation; creating forums of diverse stakeholders to generate performance breakthroughs; asking "How can this be even better?".	Resistance to change; fear of making mistakes; missed opportunities; maintaining an outdated performance culture that is driven by "This is the way this is done around here".	Change for the sake of change; lack of stability; constant jumping to the latest trend or the 'newest shiny thing'.

approaches to try. Thinking is supplemented by trying. There is a natural reluctance to attempt something unproven or without knowing for sure if it will work. The ANK is one glorious invitation to discover by trying and doing. Leaders practice and model smart experimentation. After all, amateurs built Noah's ark; professionals built the *Titanic*.

Performance Mastery Usage Indicator

We have discussed how the Performance Mastery skills are expressed and developed. Table 10 is a summary of the skills when well-used, under-used and over-used.

Summary

Performance Mastery is the leadership function that joins the three other mastery areas of relationships, vision and strategy to complete the *what* dimension of the RSVP Model. In Performance Mastery, the leader guides the transformation of plans into action, thereby continuously infusing new life into the organization. Because performance is not only about learning and adaptation but also about learning and innovation, organizations are able to thrive over the long term. Unlike the more segregated constructions of performance that delve into employee performance, operational efficiency or return on shareholder investment, in the RSVP Model, performance at the level of leadership is a collective concern that involves the leader at all three levels: the People Level, the Operational Level and the Financial Level. All stakeholders are acknowledged and rewarded for their contributions to the success of the company. Of significance is that leaders depend on employees to help them make good on their promises. In this chapter, leaders were encouraged to understand the Ten Mindsets of Performance and consider three ways of ensuring enduring performance by sustaining the positives, fixing-up the foul-ups and actualizing the possible.

Performance Mastery is the quadrant of the *Active Experimentation* Learning Style. On the Leadership Skills Profile (LSP), Performance includes the following sets of *Action Skills*:

- Setting Standards (eight o'clock)
- Taking Action (nine o'clock)
- Innovating (ten o'clock).

CHAPTER SIX

Presence Mastery

pres·ence / ˈprezəns

noun

- style of being, manner, demeanor and bearing
- ability to make one's character known to others
- physical or spiritual representation of someone or something
- the state or fact of existing

> Who you are is speaking so loudly that I can't hear what you're saying.
>
> Ralph Waldo Emerson, American essayist

Presence Mastery focuses on the engagement style of leaders as they carry forth their responsibilities. In Presence Mastery, leaders model a way of being through the effective use-of-self and the ethical exercise of power and authority. In this chapter, we discuss major facets of presence: presence across time, modes of presence, calibrating presence using Hanafin's Perceived Weirdness Index (PWI) and cultivating presence. Two sub-categories of presence are introduced: the Four Roles of Presence (experiencing, noticing, meaning-making and influencing) and the Four States of Be-ing (be-ing in love, be-ing in wisdom, be-ing in justice and be-ing in courage, which align with Relationship, Strategy, Vision and Performance). Because presence represents leadership in action, guides for practice are included throughout the chapter. This chapter concludes with a summary.

Introduction

The thinking behind the RSVP Model is that leaders must build relationships with stakeholders, identify strategic priorities, clarify a vision and inspire performance at the highest level. These tasks are the *what* of leadership – the set of essentials that drives business success. Admittedly, leaders from all types of company attend to these tasks and do them well. But many fall short. The difference lies in how they do them. We cannot emphasize enough that both *what* and *how* equate to effective leadership. *How* in this instance is not business processes and procedures or design; rather, it is the way leaders engage, communicate and connect with others. This brand of *how* requires social sensitivity. We call it presence. As American essayist Ralph Waldo Emerson implies in the opening quote, our behavior speaks louder than our words – and, we might add, louder than the tasks we undertake. Given the role that leaders play in organizations, it is easy to make the case for Presence Mastery as a fundamental of leadership.

What is Presence?

Presence binds the four 'what' components of the RSVP Model much like the connective tissue of a group of aspen trees.[52] It infuses life into the RSVP Model, making it a more holistic and integrated

---

52 According to the US National Forest Foundation, a stand or group of aspen trees is considered a singular organism, with the main life force being underground in the extensive lateral root system. Aspen is noted for its ability to regenerate vegetatively by shoots and suckers arising along its long lateral roots. Root sprouting results in many genetically identical trees, in aggregate called a 'clone'.

frame of reference. What matters in presence is use-of-self (UoS) – how leaders act upon their knowledge and experience of self, others and the world around them. More than mere technique, UoS emanates from the core of the leader and involves the thoughtful and deliberate use of experience in a way that resonates with the current situation.

Each of us has presence without further study or development. When we walk into a room, we make an impression. Presence is to a person as culture is to an organization. Both represent the way things are done. As culture is the combination of factors that are exclusive to a company, so is presence the integration of a set of characteristics that are specific to an individual. Some of these characteristics are easy to access while others are deeply embedded and must be unearthed. Once examined, choices can be made about what is beneficial and what is not. The argument is that when it comes to presence, there are no duplicates, only originals. In this regard, presence is an individual's DNA – the essence of who they are.

One of the clearest messages about presence comes from Edwin Nevis, who stressed that presence extends beyond optics and speech-making. Nevis, a Gestalt theorist and practitioner, described presence as the embodiment of all experience, knowledge, feelings, behavior, beliefs, assumptions and values that are revealed in the *stance* that one takes in a given situation.

> The practitioner is not only to stand for and express certain values, attitudes, and skills, but to use these in a way to stimulate, and perhaps evoke action necessary for movement on problems. This means that the practitioner is generally more open and revealing about their thoughts and feelings. The aim is to take advantage of the issues of difference, marginality, and

attraction to use oneself in the most powerful way possible.[53]

Indeed, presence is a form of attraction and even includes a degree of charisma. But the aim is not to harvest undying devotion from others. It is to create an atmosphere of safety and support.

Expanding the Role of Leadership

Presence has shifted its position as a competency reserved for behavioral, developmental and social-science professionals to gaining acceptance in business quarters. Those on the top rung of companies understand that formal power and stellar financial returns can take them only so far without the ability to connect with people. They are witnessing some of their rich and powerful colleagues falling from their perches because of corruption, bullying and other forms of disrespectful and unethical behavior. Today's leaders are more receptive to the idea that who they are as human beings influences their leadership. More importantly, they know that organizations are co-created, and they need followers. We tell stories of leaders declaring, "I want to work on my presence". Seldom do they know what presence is, but they can distinguish between who has presence and who does not. Much of the interest stems from their experiences with people who have left an indelible imprint on them. It is presence that gets their attention; that moves, stirs them up and leads them to say, "I want to have that effect". Moreover, they feel that a compelling presence will result not only in higher-quality connections with others but increased self-awareness. One leader explained that even though enhancing their presence means work, they are pleased to have already the resource – themselves.

Our MBA students are equally intrigued by presence. Typically, the first question at the beginning of a course on executive presence is "What is the best kind of presence for a leader to have?" And just as typically, our answer is "Yours". We say yours because there is

---

53 Nevis, 1987, p. 54.

no one best presence to have. Neither does one form of presence fit all circumstances. Having presence is having *range* – the ability to show up in a receptive way to engage with different people in different settings. Range of presence is the most important calling card for leaders in a world marked by different cultures, languages, customs and ethical standards.

When leaders are fully present, they demonstrate a capacity and capability to attend to and respond 'on demand' to emerging dynamics. This may sound like a tall order, and it is, but presence is multi-faceted. It is:

- *Complex*, because one must attend to an array of forces simultaneously

- *Effecting*, because presence makes an impact and creates shifts; it disrupts, separates and connects perspectives and people in both positive and negative ways

- *Affecting*, because the impact and shifts created by presence tap emotions and feelings, sometimes very deeply.

If we put aside whether we like a particular leader or not, we can get a better sense of what presence looks and feels like. Let us take Elon Musk, innovator, investor and multi-faceted business leader. The Tesla CEO fits the bill of dealing with complexity and is also, himself, complex. He is a polarizing figure who, quite frankly, leaves us appreciating him one day and questioning ourselves for admiring him the next, because of the positions he advocates and his in-your-face, often over-the-top behavior. But he never fails to touch our emotions in ways that are hard to ignore. Elon Musk has presence. But so does former United States First Lady Michelle Obama, who tells us, "When they go low, we go high". Her approach to managing complexity is grounding and calming; still, she challenges our thinking while tugging at our hearts. In all honesty, though the vast majority of people from around the world admire Michelle Obama, not all of them align with this particular way of thinking. We cite these two public figures to demonstrate that presence holds many personalities and perspectives. It is the reason we encourage leaders to be thoughtful about how they want to be experienced. We also urge followers to decide the leadership style that works best for them. Regardless of personality, in Presence Mastery, leaders must be honorable and curious agents of change (see Table 11).

Be Honorable
- Align personal values, attitudes, behavior
- Stand for something, take a position
- Dare to be different – or similar
- State the obvious
- Speak the unspeakable
- Lead from a base of values, morals and ethics

Be Curious
- Be interested in self
- Show genuine interest in others
- Stay in a place of perpetual wonderment
- Think always of possibilities
- Cultivate conditions for the organization to experiment with new behavior
- Continue to learn and unlearn

Be an Agent of Change
- Take care of yourself and encourage others to take care of themselves
- Use self: engage with awareness and intention
- Understand change and the importance of context
- Teach the essentials of leadership: Relationship, Strategy, Vision, Performance, Presence
- Know the difference between embracing solutions, managing dilemmas and solving problems
- Demonstrate the benefit of diversity, equity and inclusion
- Help the organization complete units of work, close unfinished business and celebrate success

Table 11. The Principles of Presence

Presence: Use-of-self with Awareness and Intention

Awareness, intention and impact drive presence. With awareness, leaders can bring consciousness to a situation – for example, of how individuals are behaving, how a team is functioning and how the company is helping and hindering itself, even disclosing something about themselves. With intention, that awareness is more structured and defined, thereby bringing purposefulness to presence. And with impact, things change. What follows are five levels of awareness, including intentional awareness, which we provide to leaders.

1. *Self-awareness* (knowing self). Those who work with others must be grounded in a mature and realistic sense of self, for without knowledge of self, knowledge of the other is much more difficult to attain. The leader's work begins with attention to self-awareness. They need to be aware of how they have been shaped by the totality of their experience. To know their tendencies, preferences, blind spots, automatic responses. To be clear about the assumptions they make, the beliefs they hold, the biases they carry and the mindsets they favor. To recognize their triggers and defaults. To own their points of view, patterns and the boundaries they set for themselves. To know what makes them comfortable and uncomfortable. In the Age of Not Knowing (ANK), leaders must learn to be comfortable being uncomfortable. They must be fully in touch with what they are feeling and thinking in the moment – and also, to be aware of what they are not aware of, what they do not notice and what they need to learn and unlearn. Our work is what we do, not who we are; but the more of who we are that we can bring to what we do, the better we will be at what we do.

2. *Social Awareness* (knowing others). Interpersonal engagement is presence because presence involves what happens when leaders interact with others. Showing interest in those in their immediate environment – seeing them, hearing them, feeling them, recognizing them. Attending to the dynamics in the room – who is communicating with whom, who is excluded, what sub-groups are present, who leads, who follows, and emerging issues of power and authority. Tracking issues of diversity, equity and inclusion, and responding appropriately. Knowing when to attend to individuals, sub-groups, the whole group or the community at large. Dealing with conflict with confidence. Determining when conflict is healthy or unhealthy.

CHAPTER SIX

Encouraging others when they are doing well and indicating their developmental needs when necessary.

3. ***Organizational Awareness*** (knowing the current state of the organization, what is needed and how to make it happen). Knowing the culture, its history, its politics, its strengths and opportunities. Scanning the organization, detecting themes, recognizing patterns, and identifying competing priorities and points of tension. Attending to when the organization makes shifts and when it is stuck, accurately assessing the forces for change and the forces for sameness (the status quo). Discerning what is present, what is missing, what is needed and what must be eliminated. Separating the bigger picture from the momentary dramas. Determining the way forward and how to get there.

4. ***Environmental Awareness*** (knowing the current and historical context of the broader environment). Placing what is taking place now in the context of its evolutionary progression. Considering the macro trends that are taking shape in the larger institutional, societal, natural, technological and global environment. During day-to-day interactions, reading the context of the particular situation and adapting accordingly based on intent. Recognizing that context matters and must be considered in determining responses, setting direction, making plans and shaping culture. Appreciating that a similar situation in a different context warrants a different response.

5. ***Intentional Awareness*** (knowing how you want to influence). Leaders sometimes react and respond automatically in ways that may not fit the occasion. Clarifying intent helps. It is conscious choice. Authors Beverly Patwell and Charlie Seashore explain that conscious choice is a better option when actions may have important implications. Their Choice Awareness Matrix is instructive in understanding the connection between awareness, the choices we make, and attribution. When leaders are aware that they are in control of their choices, they can be

accountable for what they choose. When leaders are unaware of the choices they make, their choice is automatic and habitual. When they are aware of their choices, but attribute them to others, they blame or praise others. When leaders are both unaware of the choices they make and unaware of the sources of those choices (thinking, for example, "I do not know where that came from!"), they are behaving from their socialization and inheritance (see Table 12).

Awareness	Choice Attributed to Self	Choice Attributed to Others
Leading with awareness	Holding self accountable	Blaming or praising others
Leading without awareness	Behavior is automatic and habitual	Behavior is the result of inheritance or socialization

(Patwell and Seashore, 2010)

Table 12. The Choice Awareness Matrix

Presence Across Time, Place and Space: Past, Present, Future

Generally, we speak of presence as our experience of an individual's behavior in the moment. For certain, leaders are at their best when they are fully present in the here and now, experiencing and responding to what is actually happening. But presence is much larger than 'now'. It spans time and endures. The leader who mentored us, the professor who believed in us, the elder in our neighborhood whose wise words still guide us come to mind. This form of mindshare 'outside of the now' is presence too. Peter Hawkins has a great way of capturing presence across time in his Authority, Presence, Impact Model.

Past Presence (Authority). The 'Past Presence' consists of characteristics that contribute to the leader's credibility and authority. This includes credentials, work and life experience, whom they know, positions they have held. Being able to point to other companies they have led is a platform for a new opportunity. Previous experience can set the level of gravitas perceived by others. A good example is former South African President Nelson Mandela, who generated respect and deference based on his accomplishments, history of leadership and ability to persevere in the face of seemingly insurmountable odds. His reputation preceded him and eventually elevated him to president of South Africa, Nobel Peace Prize recipient and a place of high regard across the globe.

Present Presence (Presence). Personal characteristics and ways of interacting are part of 'Present Presence'. One's appearance is high on the list because it is evident when a leader enters a room. It is not fair, but others do make judgements about how we look. For example, a leader who dresses casually in a formal environment may not be regarded as highly as one who dresses consistent with the occasion. Leaders are keenly observed to see if they measure up to expectations. The degree to which some of these qualities influence how a leader is perceived is difficult to discern because feedback at the leadership level is uncommon. We encourage leaders to ask about the impression others have of them. But appearance is not the sole component of Present Presence. It also involves what the leader does once they are in the room – how they greet, acknowledge and engage others; how they listen, communicate and facilitate conversations; how they utilize their Past Presence; and their willingness to learn.

Future Presence (Impact). Impact underlies 'Future Presence' and provides its enduring quality. It is the ability of the leader to catalyze shifts in others in the moment that will stay in their consciousness. The shift begins during the interactions but can also spring forth as an insight that emerges later. Future Presence is mindshare where something enters your mind, like an earworm,[54] without much effort on your part. Future Presence is lasting presence that leads to a desire to experience the leader again. Several questions can be used to determine a leader's Future Presence.

- In what ways did the leader shift the assumptions, thoughts and behaviors of others?
- Did the leader's values align with their behavior and with the the values of others?
- What new learning did the leader create?
- How did the leader exceed expectations?
- What curiosity did the leader evoke about what the leader might do next?
- In what ways did the leader make a lasting impression?

Modes of Presence: Evocative–Provocative, Being–Doing

As we have mentioned, presence has many manifestations before the moment, during the moment and after the moment. Some forms of presence occupy different, sometimes opposite places along a continuum – overt and covert, when speaking and when silent; when still in the room but not active; when excluding without drawing a visible boundary; when standing out without standing up; and when voting without a show of hands. Evocative and provocative presence, and being and doing presence are two continua of modes of presence.

Evocative Presence. The source is the individual, group, audience, etc. If the goal of the leader is to track what is happening and garner more information about the interest in a particular topic or situation, then they assume the evocative mode. In this mode, the leader attempts

---

54 An earworm is a catchy song or tune that runs continually through a person's mind without intentional effort on their part.

to draw out others or 'evoke' something from them. This usually occurs in the early stages of a new issue, problem or engagement. The evocative mode helps to assess other positions, thoughts, ideas and feelings. Here, the agenda is still emerging. The evocative mode creates a climate to track interest and energy. And the job is to get anchored in the situation, to stimulate conversation but not unnerve anyone. Once the direction of the work is determined, the task is to formulate a plan of action and then move to implement it. As evocateur, the leader is receptive and reflexive; uses open-ended questions, but also makes statements and comments that join and build on what is occurring rather than strongly differentiating. A safe and reassuring tone of engagement unfolds.

Provocative Presence. The source in provocative presence is the leader who leans into their more assertive presence, when this is required. True to the connotation, provocative presence is a presence that intentionally stirs others. To be provocative, the leader can assume the opposite behavior or perspective. The intent is to give the audience an alternative experience. For instance, the leader can slow the pace of a meeting with a team that moves quickly through an agenda. A provocative impact also comes from exaggerating the behavior of an audience. If the audience moves fast, the leader proceeds even faster. If only men are speaking, then the leader only acknowledges men in the room. Self as provocateur is a style that demands a response. Saying to a CEO that their behavior is inconsistent with the behavior they publicly advocate is provocative. It is probably difficult for the CEO to resist reacting to the comment. Provocative elicits a range of reactions, from surprise to slight irritation to infuriation. The idea is not to incite a riot but to stir things up. The provocative leader lives on the edge of certainty and uncertainty, never knowing what the response or reaction might be, but possessing the confidence and courage to provide a presence that support learning.

Being and Doing. Another way of looking at evocative and provocative modes of presence is along the span of being and doing. As with the evocative mode, the strength of the leader in a being orientation is to help examine situations, gain perspective, generate ideas and explore implications. The leader holds a diffuse and open awareness that is easy and unencumbered. Understanding people and their feelings is important in the being orientation. Conversely, a doing orientation is best supported by focused and structured awareness. The value of the doing orientation rests in acting and implementing plans and tasks. Achieving outcomes is the motivation. Experimenting with new behavior, testing options and experiencing different ways of working are involved. As with the provocative mode, the leader is active, taking risks and being opportunistic.

Calibrating Presence with the Perceived Weirdness Index (PWI)

Leaders are change agents. They do not just adapt to and manage change, they create it. The process involves providing something unique or rarely experienced. John Carter, scholar and co-founder of the Gestalt Organization & Systems Development Program and another one of our Gestalt teachers, always urged us to "Make a difference with your presence". Difference disrupts patterns and invites alternative ways of thinking and operating. By leveraging what is different, leaders become role models of what is possible. Disruption does not come from the good soldiers. Neither does competitive advantage. They come from the rebels, the questioners and those who are not easily satisfied with the 'right way' of doing things. The courageous leader challenges assumptions to provoke discovery.

We only have to look at the legendary country music icon Dolly Parton to see a presence that makes a difference. In early 2022, it was announced that the country singer's theme parks would pay for a college degree for their employees. Those working at Dollywood who pursue a college degree will have their tuition, associated fees and books covered in full. The offer also includes all 11,000 full-time, part-time and seasonal employees who work at any of the twenty-five amusement parks and attractions under Herschend Enterprises, Dollywood's parent company, including Dollywood. Also consider the description of Amazon founder Jeff Bezos by an executive of the

CHAPTER SIX

company: "One of the things that makes Jeff such a great leader is that his mind works differently from most others. He is constantly looking at topics from a unique angle, frequently asking Why? or Why does that have to be true? especially when he perceives that what is being presented is 'industry standard thinking.' This is why we have been able to disrupt so many different industries".

Nevertheless, difference comes with its own trials (see Figure M). Those of us who are change practitioners have long recognized the paradoxical nature of change. It is a classic experience to be sought to facilitate change but then, the minute we walk through the door, to be met with resistance. The same dynamic occurs for leaders who are hired to turn around a business or a company, only to be 'run out of town' because the organization could not tolerate a different leadership style. Neither the new leader nor the organization could bridge the gap between them. Those working in the area of diversity, equity and inclusion are familiar with, and even anticipate, the fear and rejection of difference in organizations.

"I'm right there in the room, and no one even acknowledges me."

Figure M. The Elephant in the Room

So, let us talk about how to make a difference. After all, to advance an organization, something needs to be atypical. Hanafin's Perceived Weirdness Index (PWI) is about difference and the measure of how much one is subjected to the pressure to conform in an organization. The more one conforms (a low PWI), the less likely one is to be seen or heard, or to be able to challenge the status quo. Conversely, if one is too different (a high PWI), one is apt to have a short tenure. Leaders must establish a presence that is not perceived as too weird. In his 'Rules of Thumb for Change Agents', Herb Shepard suggests that change agents should start where the system is. The aim is to locate and operate in the 'PWI sweet spot' with a presence that is similar enough, yet sufficiently different to compel the interest of others to test their assumptions, thoughts and behaviors, while feeling safe. Finding the sweet spot comes with understanding and appreciating the culture – its strengths and weaknesses – and the pace of change that it can tolerate. It comes as no surprise that diversity, equity and inclusion professionals and those who have been impacted by a company's low capacity for difference will not be comforted by a slow pace of change. Leaders must take the lead in helping to educate their companies about the dysfunction of this form of resistance to change (see Figure N).

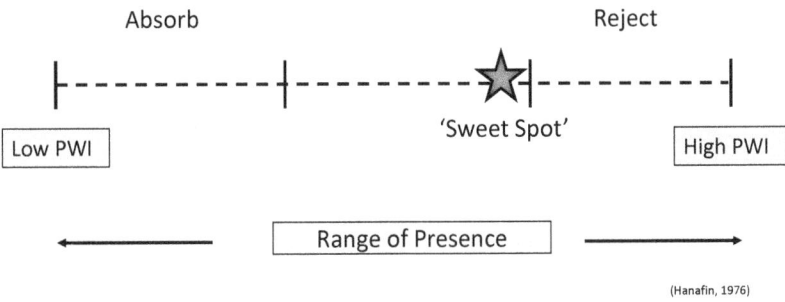

(Hanafin, 1976)

Finding the 'Sweet Spot' of Optimal Effectiveness

Figure N. The Perceived Weirdness Index (PWI)

CHAPTER SIX

Presence Mastery in Action

Presence Mastery includes two sub-categories – the Four Roles of Presence and the Four States of Be-ing that align with the Relationship, Strategy, Vision and Performance Mastery areas. The sub-categories are practical tools designed to help leaders manage the complex dynamics when in the throes of their day-to-day interactions with others.

- *The Four Roles of Presence* guide leaders in the use-of-self in four ways – experiencing, noticing, meaning-making and influencing.[55]

- *The Four States of Be-ing* encourage leaders to bring their humanity to their work through the enactment of four virtues – be-ing in love, be-ing in wisdom, be-ing in justice and be-ing in courage.

Presence in Relationship Mastery

1. *Experiencing.* Using concrete experience, experiencing involves the leader's awareness of themselves in the here and now. This requires taking inventory of internal sensations and thoughts – what they are feeling, seeing, hearing, smelling and tasting. Leaders, then, can decide how to use their experience (i.e., their use-of-self) in service of the work at hand.

The state of *be-ing in love* supports *experiencing*. When in love, leaders are aware of their heart, extending themselves, and expressing interest and affection for others and their work.

---

[55] The Four Roles of Presence is an adaptation of the Four Roles of the Gestalt Intervener, which was introduced by Claire Stratford in the Gestalt Institute of Cleveland's International Organization and Leadership Program. The Four Roles of the Gestalt Intervener is based on Dave Kolb's Experiential Learning Theory.

Presence in Strategy Mastery

2. *Meaning-making.* Using abstract conceptualization, leaders are cognizant of their thoughts, ideas and reason as they assimilate and interpret patterns and themes into useful principles, concepts and generalizations.

   The state of *be-ing in justice* supports *meaning-making*. When in justice, leaders rely on sound reasoning. They seek balance, guided by principles of fairness and equitable treatment for all.

Presence in Vision Mastery

3. *Noticing.* Using reflective observation, leaders observe others and the immediate environment, noticing and tracking themes, and recognizing patterns of behavior.

   The state of *be-ing in wisdom* supports *noticing*. When in wisdom, leaders are open to their spirit and their reservoir of life experience and 'common sense' to be rooted in soundness of perspective.

Presence in Performance Mastery

4. *Influencing.* Using active experimentation, the leader aims to create shifts and transform the system. Influencing involves intent, will and a desire to mentor, coach, advise, guide, support and motivate action.

   The state of *be-ing in courage* supports influencing. When in courage, leaders summon their confidence to triumph over fear,[56] to confront obstacles and take risks, all while rallying others and the organization to do the same.

---

[56] This reflects a quote from Nelson Mandela: "I learned that courage was not the absence of fear, but the triumph over it. The brave man is not he who does not feel afraid, but he who conquers that fear".

CHAPTER SIX

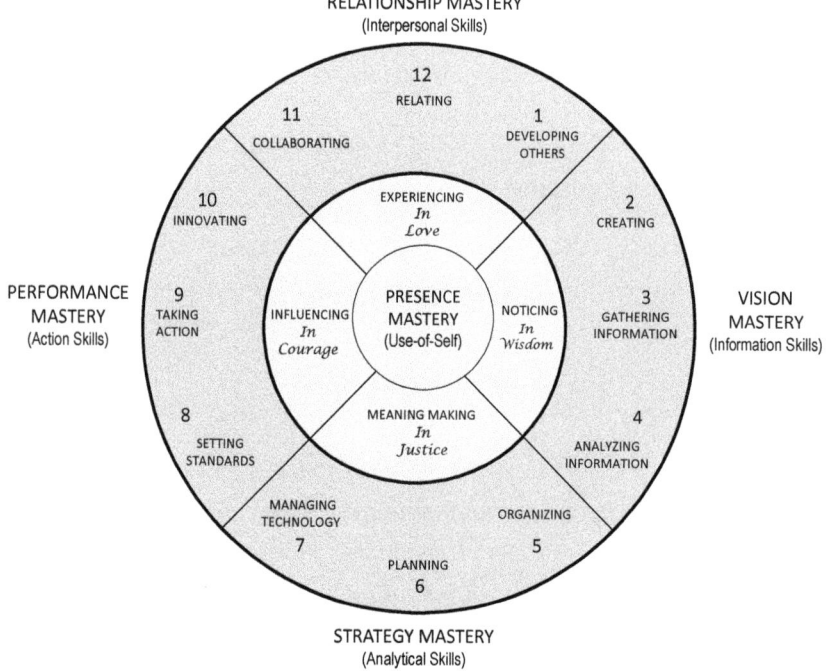

Figure O. The *What* and *How* of Leading in a Learning Way

Cultivating the Four Roles and the Four States of Be-ing of Presence

The importance of cultivating presence is captured in the quote from poet and social activist Maya Angelou, "Nothing will work unless you do". The advice is first to get your own house in order before aiming to renovate the houses of others. Here are immediate steps for leaders to develop the Four Roles of Presence and the Four States of Be-ing.[57]

---

[57] The suggestions for cultivating the Four Roles of Presence are taken from the 2009 article by Yeganeh and Kolb on mindful practice in experiential learning.

Cultivating the Four Roles of Presence

- *Developing Capacity for Experiencing.* Clearing the mind is central to engaging in present-moment experience. Deep breathing anchors the mind in immediate, here-and-now sensorial awareness of sight, sound, touch, taste and smell. Suggested practices include meditation and mindfulness, which also reduce stress, increase clarity and calmness, and improve health. Interpersonal skills such as leadership, relationship, and giving and receiving feedback can improve by developing the experiencing role.

- *Developing Capacity for Noticing.* Observing behavioral dynamics and processes without judgement or interpretation is essential. Noticing can be enhanced by deliberately viewing things from different perspectives and with empathy. Stillness and quieting the mind fosters the ability to notice. This allows patterns and themes (gestalts) to surface. Noticing expands the ability to appreciate multiple realities and engenders a natural tendency for diversity and inclusion. Information skills in pattern and theme recognition, data management and analysis can aid in noticing.

- *Developing Capacity for Meaning-making.* Questioning assumptions can help focus the mind to make 'theories-in-use' intentional rather than automatic. Taking time to view the relationship between themes and behavioral patterns can enrich grand theories. Creating contextual and relational knowledge rather than pursuing dichotomous thinking strengthens the capacity for grand theorizing. Analytical skills of theory building, data analysis and technology management can aid in the development and expression of grand theories.

- *Developing Capacity for Influencing.* In influencing, leaders move into the practical world of real consequences. Work must get done and goals must be achieved. Influencing can be enhanced by responding gracefully, without distracting from work, yet identifying what is going well and what more is needed. Leaders can develop a culture of experimentation where employees try, test and evaluate generative actions, which builds confidence and trust. Action skills, initiative, goal setting and action taking help with developing performance proficiency.

Cultivating the Four States of Be-ing of Presence

- *Developing Capacity for Be-ing in Love.* Supports Relationship Mastery and experiencing. Leading with love is being fully present in the moment with an open and extended heart toward self and those being led. Exercising an open heart involves granting the benefit of the doubt, trust as the default, modeling the strength of personal vulnerability, inviting and including, and looking for and doubling down on potential. Love is detecting and responding to pain in those we love. When in love, leaders scan the organization for policies and practices that result in human pain and suffering, and work to alleviate them. The leader's capacity for genuine self-love governs their ability to extend love. Perfection is the enemy of improvement. When in love, leaders improve with kindness and replace perfection with curiosity. John Carter teaches us that love is the most powerful force in the human experience; yet the word itself is taboo in most organizations, particularly those with male-modeled cultures. It is time to liberate leaders and acknowledge this trait we recognize in leaders we admire, follow and love. It takes courage to lead. It also takes courage to love, as fear is the opposite of love.

- *Developing Capacity for Be-ing in Justice.* Supports strategy and meaning-making. Leading when in justice is about formulating decisions based on an inclusive, equitable, honest, thorough and fair consideration of the full set of variables. All aspects are sought and weighed without regard to their convenience or favor. Be-ing in justice is about the pursuit of the right thing to do, with awareness but not prejudice regarding popular impact. Leaders in justice rely on the integrity of the deliberative process, the inclusion of all perspectives, transparency, honest consideration of facts and stakeholders feeling heard as the criteria for a good decision. Popularity, comfort and expediency may well be casualties of leading with justice. However, leaders are more than compensated for this by the priceless trust they gain for doing the right thing. Cultivating justice is enhanced by exercising intellectual rigor, cognitive flexibility, principles of perceived fairness and the pursuit of wholeness. Leaders in justice do not always feel good themselves about the decisions they must make for the good of the enterprise.[58] Leading when in justice demands that all organization processes are constantly under review for modification based on experience, for the purpose of making them more just and equitable. Such continuous improvement displays the integrity of any system.

- *Developing Capacity for Be-ing in Wisdom.* Supports noticing and vision. Leading when in wisdom is employing the broadest source of input, past and present, in the spirit of bringing all to bear on complex decision making. To gain insight, leaders scan for what is happening and not happening, noticing what is present and missing, retrieving past learning, detecting patterns and trends, organizing themes, seeking discernment. The leader in wisdom constantly strives to expand their access to the broadest range of data sources, including intuition, folklore, tradition, cross-cultural references, the latest scientific breakthroughs and embracing the richness of multiple realities. Often this means simply slowing down and being still. Wisdom is the receptor of spirit and that which is beyond the leader until it is allowed to enter. Knowing and certainty are not allies of wisdom. This suggests that leaders are better served when leaning into their curiosity. The discovery that comes with wisdom is greeted with celebration.

---

[58] Leaders who participated in our leadership survey identified the decision to terminate an employee as the most painful aspect of their job.

- *Developing Capacity for Be-ing in Courage.* Supports performance and influencing. Leading when in courage is about staring into the abyss and moving ahead with action despite the uncertainties involved. With no clear or best path, leaders draw confidence from thorough efforts to forecast, calibrate, assess and project obstacles and likely outcomes. Be-ing in courage requires a sense of preparedness for the unanticipated and trust in self and others. The delusion of control yields to the humility and courage of improvisation. Belief in the ability to adapt can be drawn from the record of accomplishment of past successes. Or it may just as likely be pulled from an inner faith that success will arrive when needed. Fear is useful as far as it is an alert to dangers ahead and courage is the antidote to fear. Courage enables leaders to take the plunge with confidence and resolve. Leading when in courage draws on humanity's determination to put forth the best effort to assure survival and a quality of life.

Summary

The purpose of this chapter is to encourage leaders to develop a more powerful presence. Relationship, strategy, vision and performance represent *what* leaders do. Presence is the *how*, the connective tissue that binds the four fundamentals and delivers balance to the practice of leadership. Presence is use-of-self with awareness and intention. Everyone has presence but leaders can benefit from calibrating and cultivating their presence. When effective, leaders have access to their range of presence – past, present and future; however, the ability to be fully in the moment, experiencing and responding to what is actually happening is the mark of excellence. Modes of presence – evocative or provocative, being or doing – were discussed here to help leaders make choices about how they wish to be experienced. They can also learn to calibrate their presence using the Perceived Weirdness Index.

We introduced the Four Roles of Presence and the Four States of Be-ing as tools for presence in action:

- With the *Four Roles of Presence* – experiencing, noticing, making-meaning and influencing – leaders bring their heart, spirit, mind and body to work.

- The *Four States of Be-ing of Presence* – be-ing in love, be-ing in wisdom, be-ing in justice and be-ing in courage – allow leaders to bring their humanity as well.

PART III

ONWARD

CHAPTER SEVEN

Learning for the Future of Leadership

What We Did

We decided to author a book about leadership because a major part of people's daily needs and activities are affected by organizations and those who lead them. But the context of organizations today is constantly changing, leaving leaders at a loss as to what to do in what we refer to as the Age of Not Knowing. With the knowledge that both learning and leading are adaptive processes, we applied Experiential Learning Theory and Gestalt theory and practice to leadership and integrated them with prevailing research, theory and principles of leadership. We are confident in our framework for leading in a learning way – the Relationship Strategy Vision Performance Fundamentals of Leadership (RSVP) Model. It is distinct in its holistic examination of both the *what* and the *how* of leadership.

How We Did It

Our approach to the book was to establish a backdrop with the opening chapters – Understanding Context, Understanding Change, Understanding Leadership, and Understanding Leadership and Learning. These beginning discussions were followed by chapters on each of the five mastery areas of the RSVP Model – Relationship

Mastery, Strategy Mastery, Vision Mastery, Performance Mastery and Presence Mastery – how they are manifested in the leader's work life, the specific skill sets associated with each mastery area and how the skills are developed.

Developing Leaders for the Future

Because leading from learning is a paradigm shift, developmental strategies are necessary. Every leader has a distinct approach to both learning and leading that is further impacted by their company's culture. Application of the RSVP Model varies depending on the personal style and skill of the leader, combined with the demands of their jobs. A technology-driven company might require a higher level of leader competence in strategy and performance while a non-governmental organization might emphasize vision and relationships. Still, the other mastery areas must not be overlooked because they, too, are critical to healthy organizational functioning. Leaders must ensure that all mastery areas are attended to by someone on their immediate team.

1. *Learning Style.* Determine the leader's learning style to establish the emphasis placed[59] on each of the four learning modes: Concrete Experience, Reflective Observation, Abstract Conceptualization and Active Experimentation.

2. *Identify RSVP Developmental Opportunities.* To translate learning styles into leading skills, we identified and operationalized 36 proficiencies for the RSVP Model, nine for each mastery area.

    o Using a Likert Scale (1–7), the leader's *Strengths* can be identified for each skill.

---

59 Dave Kolb and Richard Boyatzis identified 72 executive skills in their assessment instrument, the Executive Skills Profile, that translated learning styles into learning skills. See Boyatzis and Kolb, 1995.

o The same Likert Scale (1–7) can be used to assess the leader's *Job Demands*.

o The gap between the rating of *Strengths* and *Job Demands* reveals *Developmental Opportunities*.

o A plan for development is created. Executive coaching and training are development strategies.

3. ***Presence.*** Developmental strategies for presence include:

o Gestalt Personal Growth workshops, NTL Institute's Human Interaction Laboratory

o Courses in mindfulness, awareness, yoga, etc.

o Presence workshops

o Training in coaching

o Training in working with groups

o Training in facilitating large groups.

The Qualities for Learning for the Future of Leadership

One of our goals is to elevate the next generation of leaders by debunking the myth of the all-knowing leader and help leaders see the value in embracing continuous learning. Leading from a learning stance is the most reliable risk that leaders can take into the future. But they must adhere to a set of qualities that often sit outside the mainstream of assumptions about leadership – holism, systemic, integrative, alignment, generativity, inquiry, emergence and awareness.

Holism. Aristotle captured the idea of holism in his statement, "the whole is more than the sum of the parts", which is in contrast to reductionism that breaks things down into their smallest parts. The term 'holism' was coined in 1926 by South African Jan Smuts. It is derived from Ancient Greek *holos* ὅλος, meaning 'all, whole, entire, total'. Smuts believed that evolution pushed humans and societies to join even larger wholes, culminating for instance in global forms of society like the League of Nations, which he was instrumental in forming. Though a segregationist in his own country, his philosophical perspectives on holism are widely accepted. When it comes to leadership, holism means that it is not enough to focus on a single component. The full set of forces, individuals and parts, immediate and distant, must be seen and seen simultaneously. Consequently, the leader's work becomes an on-going process of diversity and inclusion.

Systemic. Holism also suggests a systems view of all parts, internal and external, the relationship between the parts and how they have influenced and influence each other. Just as important is the principle of boundaries and boundary management. If the boundaries are not managed to allow the best flow of inputs and outputs, the company becomes vulnerable to the negative side of self-reliance or reliance on the environment. A systems lens also keeps leaders attuned to the dynamic nature of the environment and its impact on the life of the organization. But more than knowledge of the outside world is needed for survival. Structures that support quick and effective responses have proven to be indispensable for success.

Integrative. It follows that if learning leadership is holistic and systemic, it must too be integrative, spanning many domains. Integration arises from the seamless coordination and alignment of people, functions and processes. Integration is like jazz in that what we hear in jazz is the improvisational coming together of the instruments. When the need arises, a particular instrument can be showcased and then rejoin the ensemble. In organizations, the major functional areas represent the instruments. At the individual level, integration is the seamless mix of aspects of the self – affective, perceptual, cognitive and behavioral.

Alignment. The power of alignment is seldom recognized as a critical part of leadership practice. Many companies have a checklist of items that are essential to success, yet never invest the time to synchronize those items. Then, they wonder why people are confused and support is absent. Once the bigger picture is in view, the parts must 'hang together'. Purpose must drive vision which informs the strategic priorities. Values, ethics and rewards guide how those priorities will be implemented. You will not get a team culture if bonuses are based on individual achievements, and vice versa. It simply is not possible. And alignment is more than a concept; it is collective action. All members of the leadership team should agree about the way forward and communicate the same message. Employees will come to trust leadership when there is consistency – they will hear, see and feel how the parts of the puzzle fit together. Soon employees themselves will be passing the messages on to other employees and the desired culture will begin to take shape. Furthermore, those outside the organization will notice that everyone sings from the same song book. Alignment provides the entire organization with something to get behind and gives observers something to admire.

Inquiry. Unlike the cat, curiosity will not kill us.[60] Rather, it will propel organizations into another era of creativity, growth and abundance. Curiosity plays a major role in inquiry-based learning – the real-world learning that is characterized by exploration and high-level questioning through engagement and interaction with others. Leveraging personal interest in a topic or subjects reinforces commitment to inquiry. At the level of leadership, inquiry-based learning places the leader, the organization and member engagement at the center of exploration of the future. The idea is present-day investigation of potential, opportunity and things hoped for.

Generativity. Learning begets learning, engages the imagination, stimulates fresh ideas and foretells new possibilities and transformations. In a generative culture, historic assumptions are challenged – assumptions about what the work is, how it gets done and who does it. Generative leadership presumes inquiry, collaboration,

---

60 The proverb 'curiosity killed the cat' is used to attempt to stop someone asking too many questions.

conversation and experimentation. Organizational transformation is the objective as new ideas are welcomed and implemented.

Emergence. Here we are emphasizing again the importance of the *how* of leadership that is propelled by the leader's presence. The end to non-stop change is not forthcoming any time soon. Fortunately, the principles of adaptive change have helped leaders reimagine and prepare for unanticipated change. We regard unanticipated change more broadly as *emergent change.* Emergence applies not only to dynamics outside the organization. What must be considered are the day-to-day, in-the-moment human dynamics that also require adaptive ability. Conventional portrayals of leadership exclude the 'real' nature of the leader's role: relationship building, engaging others and the collaborative efforts that are needed to get work done. With skill and competence in responding to all forms of emergent change, leaders develop an appetite for the excitement of the unknown that the future holds and have the confidence that whatever arises, they can handle it.

Awareness. Presence involves the ability to work in the here and now. Leaders must have an active state of awareness. Consciously knowing in the moment is one way to describe awareness. They must be aware, first, of themselves to monitor their energy, moods, biases and trigger points. Next, they must be aware of others and the broader environment. Finally, given this internal and external scanning, leaders are better informed about how to respond. Carrying this inward and outward consciousness is helpful during times of crisis when everyone is feeling the stress of work, including the leader.

Where to in the Future

Beyond Learning and Adaptation to Innovation. We challenge leaders to go beyond adaptation to innovation. That is also a message to the two of us. Our next horizon is one that should expound more fully on the merits of innovation. We are keenly interested in elaborating more about going beyond learning and adaptation to learning and innovation. There is a growing realization that even the comfort of adaptive processes is insufficient in the face of the sheer magnitude of complexity that the world is facing. Out of a need for survival, leaders must not only leverage learning by reflecting on past experience and adapting but also extract implications for cutting-edge products and services. Relationships, vision, strategy, performance and presence remain relevant, they just have a broader scope in time. Ways of utilizing the mastery areas for innovation must be created from the ground up. Of course, leaders must adjust their systems to align more with the external forces impacting their organizations. This is true whether the impetus is changing climate, customer needs, politics, social issues, government, global markets or competition.

Adaptation is a more reactive response that often relies on what has gone before and what is known. On the other hand, innovation is the translation of creativity into something positive that has never been done before. A few things are necessary to include innovation as part of the leader's role.

About Innovation

- Innovation is creating and producing something that has not been produced before.
- Innovation aims to impact the industry and exceed customer expectations.
- Innovation begins with and transforms creativity into a product or service.
- Innovation carries risks and requires investment of talent, time and money.

According to the Center for Creative Leadership, innovation is *new pieces coming together with old pieces in new ways.*

About the Innovative Leader

We define an innovative leader as a leader who guides individuals, groups and the organization in the use of healthy, cutting-edge behaviors to blaze new trails, create new products and services in a complex environment.

- An innovative leader recognizes the ever-fluctuating nature of business and can quickly react to new challenges and circumstances.

- An innovative leader also goes one step further, anticipating challenges before they arise and taking proactive measures to face them.

- An innovative leader is driven to understand people and the company's operating context.

- An innovative leader accepts what is really happening as opposed to what they want to happen.

- An innovative leader believes in continuous improvement, individually and organizationally.

- An innovative leader acknowledges the need for personal, group and organization development for innovation to flourish, seeking and building the necessary skills, regardless of the discomfort this development may impose.

- An innovative leader understands that adequate resources and reward systems must be committed to sustain an innovative culture.

- An innovative leader is open to learning in multiple ways and for multiple purposes.

Diversity, Equity and Inclusion. The most urgent topic for further study is DEI and the leader's role in creating and sustaining more diverse, equitable and inclusive systems. This would require more of both qualitative (to understand people's experience) and quantitative (reliable and valid) research because we simply do not know enough about leadership and diversity: specifically, the experience of diverse leaders (leading while different), the task of leadership in designing and maintaining diverse cultures (more leader accountability) and the complex dynamic of diversity, power and authority.

Further Study of the RSVP Model. Our current work constantly stimulates, refining and extending the power of the RSVP Model. There are many more illustrations available from our experience that warrant sharing.

- We may well be unable to resist converting the RSVP Model into a leadership development tool. The attraction of taking what we have created and enabling clients to develop their leadership of the future feels irresistible.

- It would be useful to further explore the interplay of the five aspects – Relationship Mastery, Strategy Mastery, Vision Mastery, Performance Mastery and Presence Mastery. For example, in what ways does the grasping function that feeds the relationships detract from being strategic? How does someone's presence impact their ability to perform? How does the vision of a compelling future come to die a quiet death in the absence of the relationship capability that enables others to embrace it?

What We Invite You to Do for Our Future

So many cutting-edge ideas are floating around in schools, in companies (large and small), among practitioners and in family systems that stimulate thought about the future of organizations and leadership. Our bet is that your ideas are among them. We take issue with pundits who in order to legitimize their ideas, dismiss or appropriate the work of others. Leadership and learning are big tents with room for many. The more we have and the more diverse the thoughts, the richer the discourse and the better is our collective understanding. Continue to stay abreast of what is happening in companies so that we can help them be more humane and become bastions of inclusivity and justice and not solely focused on profit at any cost. We stepped into the fray and now invite you to research, learn and share your insights about leadership and learning.

Differences exist among approaches to leadership but what is seldom disputed and what they have in common is that leadership is nothing without people; that leadership must be guided by some sense of purpose and vision, regardless of who does the leading or when it is done; priorities must be identified, planned and established, and the work that is promised and expected must be delivered.

It took time for us to reach these back pages. In our preface, we said that this book was brutal. And now that it is done, we also say that it has been a very satisfying experience.

BIBLIOGRAPHY

Ashford, S.J., and DeRue, D.S. (2012) 'Developing as a leader: The power of mindful engagement', *Organizational Dynamics* 41(2): 146–154.

Barrett, F.J. (2017) 'The social construction of organizing', in D.B. Szabla, W.A. Pasmore, M.A. Barnes and A.N. Gipson (eds), *The Palgrave Handbook of Organizational Change Thinkers*. Palgrave Macmillan Cham. https://doi.org/10.1007/978-3-319-52878-6_101

Barton, D., Grant, A., and Horn, M. (2012) 'Six global leaders confront the personal and professional challenges of a new era of uncertainty', *McKinsey Quarterly* (June). www.mckinsey.com/insights/leadinginthe21stcentury

Bathiwala, S. (2011) *Feminist Leadership for Social Change: Clearing the Conceptual Cloud*. CREA.

Beisser, A. (1970) 'The paradoxical theory of change', in J. Fagan and L. Shepherd (eds), *Gestalt Therapy Now*. Science and Behavior Books.

Blackerby, P. (2003) 'History of strategic planning'. http://www.blackerbyassoc.com/history.html [retrieved 22 March 2017].

Block, P. (2008) 'Leadership and the small group', *Training & Development* (T+D) (July), published by the American Society for Training and Development (ASTD), pp. 40–43.

Block, P. (2018) *Community: The Structure of Belonging* (2nd ed.). Berrett-Koehler.

Bohns, V. (2021) *You Have More Influence than You Think: How We Underestimate Our Power of Persuasion, and Why it Matters.* W.W. Norton & Company.

Boyatzis, R.E., and Kolb, D.A. (1991) *Learning Skills Profile.* Hay/McBer Training Resources Group.

Boyatzis, R.E., and Kolb, D.A. (1995) 'From learning styles to learning skills: The executive skills profile', *Journal of Managerial Psychology* 10(5): 3–17.

Boyatzis, R.E., and Kolb, D.A. (1997) 'Assessing individuality in learning: The learning skills profile', *Educational Psychology* 11(3–4): 279–295.

Brady, D. (Host) (2021) 'The search for purpose at work: Purpose is personal, but companies play a critical role in how we express it' [Audio podcast episode], *The McKinsey Podcast* (3 June), McKinsey & Company. https://www.mckinsey.com/capabilities/people-and-organizational-performance/our-insights/the-search-for-purpose-at-work

Branden, N. (2001) *The Psychology of Self-esteem* (32nd anniversary ed.). Jossey-Bass.

Brewer, M.B. (1991) 'The social self: On being the same and different at the same time', *Personality and Social Psychology Bulletin* 17: 475–482.

Brickhouse, T.C., and Smith, N.D. (1994) *Plato's Socrates.* Oxford University Press.

Brown, B. (2018) *Dare to Lead: Brave Work, Tough Conversations, Whole Hearts.* Vermillion.

Buckingham, M., and Goodall, A. (2019) 'The feedback fallacy', *Harvard Business Review* (March–April), 92–101. https://hbr.org/2019/03/the-feedback-fallacy

Burns, J.M. (1978) *Leadership.* Harper & Row.

Carter, J. D. & GestaltOSD Center. (2020). *Making a Difference With Your Presence: Use of Self and Self Mastery.* River Place Press.

Carter, J.D., Rainey Tolbert, M.A., and Blair, M. (eds) (2004) *Organization Development and Gestalt: An Ongoing Partnership, OD Practitioner* 36(4) [special edition].

Cheung-Judge, M., and Holbeche, L. (2015) *Organization Development: A Practitioner's Guide for OD and HR*. Kogan Page.

Chidiac, M.A. (2018) *Relational Organisational Gestalt: An Emergent Approach to Organisation Development*. Routledge.

Cole Rachel, T. (2022) 'Selling the Drama: A conversation with Lin-Manuel Miranda on theatre, creativity and the endless regenerative power of New York City', *Departures* (3 May). https://www.departures.com/arts/lin-manuel-miranda-interview-nyc?extlink=em-us-dp-sfmcmail19-body-1-linnyc-0

Cooperrider, D., Rainey Sharp, M.A., Tenkasi, R., and Wilmot, T. (1989) 'The TRW manager of volunteers program: An evaluation study'. Case Western Reserve University, Weatherhead School of Management. Unpublished document.

Cowie, K. (2012) *Finding Merlin: A Handbook for the Human Development Journey in Our New Organisational World*. Marshall Cavendish Business.

Dixon-Fyle, S., Hunt, V., Dolan, K., and Prince, S. (2020) 'Diversity wins: How inclusion matters'. McKinsey & Company. https://www.mckinsey.com/~/media/mckinsey/featured%20insights/diversity%20and%20inclusion/diversity%20wins%20how%20inclusion%20matters/diversity-wins-how-inclusion-matters-vf.pdf [retrieved 14 June 2021].

Dweck, C.S. (2007) *Mindset: The New Psychology of Success*. Random House.

Dweck, C.S. (2017) *Mindset: Changing the Way You Think to Fulfill Your Potential*. Robinson.

Dyer, W.W. (2013) *The Essential Wayne Dyer Collection*. Hay House Inc.

Edmondson, A. (1999) 'Psychological safety and learning behavior in work teams', *Administrative Science Quarterly* 44(2): 350–383. https://doi.org/10.2307/2666999

Esimai, C. (2019) 'Great leadership starts with self-awareness' (15 February). https://www.forbes.com/sites/ellevate/2018/02/15/self-awareness-being more-of-what-makes-you-great

Eubank, D., Geffken, D., Orzano, J., and Ricci, R. (2012) 'Teaching adaptive leadership to family medicine residents: What? Why? How?' *Families Systems & Health* 30(3): 241–252.

Fink, L. (2012) 'Leading in the 21st century: An interview with Larry Fink, chairman and CEO, BlackRock', *McKinsey Quarterly: The Online Journal of McKinsey & Company* (September): 1–6.

Freire, P. (1974) *Pedagogy of the Oppressed*. Continuum.

Furedi, F. (2018) *How Fear Works: Culture of Fear in the 21st Century*. Bloomsbury Continuum.

Gold, M. (ed.) (1999) *The Complete Social Scientist: A Kurt Lewin Reader*. American Psychological Association.

Goleman, D. (1995) *Emotional Intelligence: Why It Can Matter More than IQ*. Bantam Books.

Greenleaf, R.K. (1970) *The Servant as Leader*. Robert K. Greenleaf Publishing Center.

Hanafin, J. (1976) 'PWI --- The perceived weirdness index'. (Educational document). Syncrude Canada Ltd.

Hanafin, J. (2004) 'Rules of thumb for awareness agents', *Organization Development Practitioner* 36(4): 24–28.

Hanafin, J. (2012) 'Problems and dilemmas'. Client briefing, Jonno Hanafin Associates.

Hanafin, J., and Rainey, M.A. (2020) 'The learning/acceptance ratio in response to change' (PowerPoint slide). The iGOLD Program III Interim Virtual Session.

Haslam, S.A., Reicher, S.D., and Platow, M.J. (2020) *The New Psychology of Leadership: Identity, Influence and Power* (2nd ed.). Routledge.

Hawkins, P., and Smith, N. (2006) *Coaching, Mentoring and Organizational Consultancy: Supervision and Development* (1st ed.). Open University Press/McGraw-Hill.

Heifetz, R., and Laurie, D. (2001) 'The work of leadership', *Harvard Business Review* (December).

Hoffer, E. (1973) *Reflections of the Human Condition*. Restored to print by C. Klim, 2006. Hopewell Publications.

Horney, K. (1950) *Neurosis and Human Growth: The Struggle Toward Self-realization*. W.W. Norton.

January-Bardill, N.J. (ed.) (2021) *Write to Speak: A Collection of Stories Written by African Women Leaders*. Bardill & Associates.

Johnson, B. (1992) *Polarity Management: Identifying and Managing Unsolvable Problems*. HRD Press.

Jourard, S.M. (1971) *The Transparent Self*. Van Nostrand Reinhold.

Jung, C.G. (1971) 'The collected works of C.G. Jung', in J. Campbell (ed.), *The Portable Jung*. Viking Press. (Original work published, 1921; original translation, 1923.)

Kaplan, R.S., and Norton, D.P. (1992) 'The balanced scorecard – Measures that drive performance', *Harvard Business Review* (January–February): 1–18. https://hbr.org/1992/01/the-balanced-scorecard-measures-that-drive-performance-2

Kelly, Nataly (2018) 'Research Shows Immigrants Help Businesses Grow: Here's Why', *Harvard Business Review* (26 October). https://hbr.org/2018/10/research-shows-immigrants-help-businesses-grow-heres-why

Kolb, D.A. (2015) *Experiential Learning: Experience as the Source of Learning and Development* (2nd ed.). Pearson Education. [Original published 1984 by Prentice-Hall.]

Kolb, A.Y., and Kolb, D.A. (2011) 'Learning Style Inventory Version 4.0', Korn Ferry/Hay Group. http://store.kornferry.com/store/lominger/en_us/list/categoryID_4836644000/parentCategoryID.4836643700

Kolb, A.Y., and Kolb, D.A. (2017) *The Experiential Educator: Principles and Practices of Experiential Learning*. EBLS Press.

Kotter, J.P. (1990) *A Force for Change: How Leadership Differs from Management*. The Free Press.

Kouzes, J.M., and Posner, B.Z. (2016) *Learning Leadership: The Five Fundamentals of Becoming an Exemplary Leader*. Wiley.

Krech, G. (2022) 'Manage energy, not time', in *Thirty Thousand Days: A Journal for Purposeful Living* (August). ToDo Institute. https://www.thirtythousanddays.org/2022/08/karoshi-manage-energy-not-time/

Kriegel, R., and Brandt, D. (1996) *Sacred Cows Make the Best Burgers: Developing Change-driving People and Organizations.* Warner Books.

Leary-Joyce, J. (2014) *The Fertile Void: Gestalt Coaching at Work.* AOEC Press.

Leonard, G. (1992) *Mastery: The Keys to Success and Long-term Fulfillment.* Plume.

Lewin, K. (1952) *Field Theory in Social Science: Selected Theoretical Papers by Kurt Lewin.* London: Tavistock.

Lewin, K. (1997) *Resolving Social Conflicts & Field Theory in Social Science.* American Psychological Association.

Lewin, K. (1999) *The Complete Social Scientist.* American Psychological Association.

Luthans, F., and Peterson, S.J. (2004) '360-degree feedback with systematic coaching: Empirical analysis suggests a winning combination', *Human Resource Management* 42(3): 243–256. https://doi.org/10.1002/hrm.10083

MacIntyre, A. (2007) *After Virtue: A Study in Moral Theory* (3rd ed.). University of Notre Dame Press.

Marrow, A.J. (1969) *The Practical Theorist: The Life and Work of Kurt Lewin.* Basic Books.

Maslow, A.H. (1943) 'A theory of human motivation', *Psychological Review* 50: 370–396.

McLaren, P., and Leonard, P. (eds) (1993) *Paulo Freire: A Critical Encounter.* Routledge.

McLeod, S. (2008) 'Self concept', Simply Psychology. www.simplypsychology.org/self-concept.html

Mead, G.H. (1982) *The Individual and the Social Self: Unpublished Work of George Herbert Mead* (edited by David L. Miller). University of Chicago Press.

Mead, G.H. (2015) *Mind, Self & Society: The Definitive Edition* (edited by Charles W. Morris; annotated edition by Daniel R. Huebner and Hans Joas). University of Chicago Press.

Mintzberg, H. (1994) 'The fall and rise of strategic planning of organizations: A synthesis of the research', *Harvard Business Review* (January–February): 107–115.

Moingeon, B., and Edmondson, A. (eds) (1996) *Organizational Learning and Competitive Advantage*. Sage Publications.

Montgomery, C. (2012) 'How strategists lead', *McKinsey Quarterly: The Online Journal of McKinsey & Company* (1 July): 2–7. https://www.mckinsey.com/business-functions/strategy-and-corporate-finance/our-insights/how-strategists-lead

Morgan, G. (2006) *Images of Organization*. Sage Publications.

Nevis, E.C. (1987) *Organizational Consulting: A Gestalt approach*. Gardner Press.

Nevis, E.C., Hanafin, J., and Rainey Tolbert, M.A. (2006) 'Working with individuals in an organizational context', in B.B. Jones and M. Brazzel (eds), *The NTL Handbook of Organization Development and Change: Principles, Practices, Perspectives* (pp. 249–263). Pfeiffer.

Nevis, E.C., Hanafin, J., and Rainey, M.A. (2014) 'Working with individuals in organizations: Coaching, facilitating interaction with others, and strategic advising', in B.B. Jones and M. Brazzel (eds), *The NTL Handbook of Organization Development and Change: Principles, Practices, Perspectives* (2nd ed., pp. 429–443). Wiley.

Nevis, S.M., Backman, S., and Nevis, E.C. (2003) 'Connecting strategic and intimate interactions: The need for balance', *Gestalt Review* 7(2): 134–146.

Newman, M. (2017) 'Emotional Capitalists – Leaders of Innovation', YouTube (31 July). https://www.youtube.com/watch?v=LzB1vg7YSp4

Nowlen, P.M. (1988) *A New Approach to Continuing Education for Business and the Professions*. McMillan.

Papp, K. (2015) 'Rev up your thinking skills by trying something new', Harvard Health Online (December). https://www.health.harvard.edu/healthy-aging/rev-up-your-thinking-skills-by-trying-something-new

Patwell, B., and Seashore, E.W. (2010) *Triple Impact Coaching: Use of Self in the Coaching Process* (2nd ed.). Victoria, BC, Canada: Patwell Consulting. c06.indd 125.

Pearce, C.L., and Conger, J.A. (2003) *Shared Leadership: Reframing the Hows and Whys of Leadership.* Sage Publications.

Peres, S. (2012) 'Leading in the 21st century: An interview with Shimon Peres, President of Israel', *McKinsey Quarterly: The Online Journal of McKinsey & Company* (September): 1–4. https://www.mckinsey.com/~/media/McKinsey/Featured%20Insights/Leading%20in%20the%2021st%20Century/An%20interview%20with%20Shimon%20Peres/Shimon_Peres.pdf

Perlman, D. (2007) 'The best of times, the worst of times: The place of close relationships in psychology and our daily lives', *Canadian Psychology* 48(1): 7–18.

Perlman, H.H. (1979) *Relationship: The Heart of Helping People.* University of Chicago Press.

Perls, F.S. (1947) *Ego, Hunger and Aggression.* Gestalt Journal Press.

Perls, F.S., Hefferline, R., and Goodman, P. (1951) *Gestalt Therapy.* Julian Press.

Peterson, K., and Kolb, D.A. (2017) *How You Learn is How You Live: Using Nine Ways of Learning to Transform Your Life.* Berrett-Koehler.

Pfeiffer, J.W. (1986) 'Appendix: The history of strategic planning', in J.W. Pfeiffer (ed.), *Strategic Planning: Selected Readings* (pp. 501–513). University Associates.

Rainey, M.A. (1996) 'An appreciative inquiry into the factors of culture continuity during leadership transition: A case study of LeadShare, Canada', *OD Practitioner* 28(1&2): 34–42.

Rainey, M.A. (2004) 'Gestalt therapy theory and transformational leadership: A commentary... of sorts', *Gestalt Review* (10)2.

Rainey, M.A. (2014) 'Kurt Lewin: Some reflections', in B.B. Jones and M. Brazzel (eds), *The NTL Handbook of Organization Development and Change: Principles, Practices, Perspectives* (2nd ed., pp. 643–648). Wiley.

Rainey, M.A. (2019) 'Four roles of the Gestalt intervener: Holistic presence using experiential learning theory', in M.A. Rainey and B.B. Jones (eds), *Gestalt Practice: Living and Working in Pursuit of wHolism* (pp. 59–73). Libri.

Rainey, M.A., Hekelman, F., Galazka, S.F., and Kolb, D.A. (1993) 'Job demands and personal skills in family medicine: Implications for faculty development', *Family Medicine* 25: 100–103.

Rainey, M.A., and Jones, B. (2014) 'Use of self as an OD Practitioner', in B.B. Jones and M. Brazzel (eds), *The NTL Handbook of Organization Development and Change: Principles, Practices, Perspectives* (2nd ed., pp. 105–126). Wiley.

Rainey, M.A., and Jones, B.B. (eds) (2019) *Gestalt Practice: Living and Working in Pursuit of wHolism*. Libri.

Rainey, M.A., and Kolb, D.A. (1995) 'Using experiential learning theory and learning styles in diversity education', in R.R. Sims and S.J. Sims (eds), *The Importance of Learning Styles: Understanding the Implications for Learning, Course Design, and Education* (pp. 129–146). Greenwood Press.

Rainey, M.A., and Kolb, D.A. (2014) 'Organizational leadership: Leading in a learning way', in B.B. Jones and M. Brazzel (eds), *The NTL Handbook of Organization Development and Change: Principles, Practices, Perspectives* (2nd ed., pp. 329–347). Wiley.

Rainey, M.A., and Stratford, C. (2001) 'Reframing resistance to change: A Gestalt perspective', in G. Bermann and G. Meurer (eds), *Best Patterns – Erfolgsmuster fur Zukunftsfahiges Management* (pp. 327–336). Hemnn Luchterhand Verlag, GmbH. Neuwied und Kriftel.

Rainey Sharp, M.A. (1991) 'Career development in academic family medicine: An experiential learning approach'. Doctoral dissertation, Case Western Reserve University.

Rainey Tolbert, M.A. (2004) 'What is Gestalt organization & systems development? All about the O, the S, the D... and of course, Gestalt', *OD Practitioner* 36(4): 6–10.

Rainey Tolbert, M.A., and Hanafin, J. (2006) 'Use-of-self in OD consulting: What matters is presence', in B.B. Jones and M. Brazzel (eds), *The NTL Handbook of Organization Development and Change: Principles, Practices, Perspectives* (pp. 69–82). Pfeiffer.

Roethlisberger, F.J., and Dickson, W. (1939) *Management and the Worker: An Account of a Research Program Conducted by the Western Electric Company, Hawthorne Works, Chicago.* Harvard University Press.

Rozovsky, J. (2015) 'The five keys to a successful Google team', re:Work (17 November). https://rework.withgoogle.com/blog/five-keys-to-a-successful-google-team/

Seashore, C., Shawver, M.N., Thompson, G., and Mattare, M. (2004) 'Doing good by knowing who you are: The instrumental self as an agent of change', *OD Practitioner* 36(3): 42–46.

Seijts, G.H., and Latham, G.P. (2005) 'Learning versus performing goals: When should each be used?' *Academy of Management Executive* 19: 124–131.

Senge, P. (1990) *The Fifth Discipline: The Art and Practice of the Learning Organization.* Currency/Doubleday.

Siminovitch, D.E. (2017) *A Gestalt Primer: The Path toward Awareness IQ.* Gestalt Coaching Works, LLC.

Simpson, C.R. (1984) 'A conversation, not a monologue', *The Chronicle of Higher Education*, pull-out section (16 March), p. 2.

Sims, R.R., and Sims, S.J. (eds) (1995) *The Importance of Learning Styles: Understanding the Implications for Learning, Course Design, and Education.* Greenwood Press.

Smith, M.K. (2008) 'Helping relationships', The Encyclopedia of Pedagogy and Informal Education. www.infed.org/mobi/helping-relationships-principles-theory-and-practice/ [retrieved 25 March 2022].

Snodgrass, G.A., Rainey, M.A., and Gupta, S. (2001) 'Lessons for leadership from a merger of equals'. Internal executive brief, Exelon Corporation.

Staats, B.R. (2018) *Never Stop Learning: Stay Relevant, Reinvent Yourself and Thrive.* Harvard Business Review Press.

Takeuchi, H., Osono, E., and Shimizu, N. (2008) 'The Contradictions That Drive Toyota's Success', *Harvard Business Review* (June). https://hbr.org/2008/06/the-contradictions-that-drive-toyotas-success

Tannenbaum, R.T., and Hanna, R.W. (1985) 'Holding on, letting go, and moving on: Understanding a neglected perspective on change', in R.T. Tannenbaum, N. Margulies and F. Massarik (eds), *Human Systems Development*. Jossey-Bass.

Taylor, C. (1992) *Multiculturalism and 'The Politics of Recognition': An Essay with Commentary*. Princeton University Press.

Taylor, F.W. (1911) *Principles of Scientific Management*. Harper and Brothers.

Webmaster (2022) 'List of Fortune 500 companies and their websites'. http://www.zyxware.com/articles/4344/list-of-fortune-500-companies-and-their-websites [retrieved 22 March 2017].

Wilson, A.L., and Hayes, E.R. (2002) 'From the Editors: The problem of (learning in-from-to experience) experience', *Adult Education Quarterly* 52(3): 173–175.

Woyzbun, R.P. (no date) 'The evolution of strategic planning', *The/ Marketing/Works* 1–8. http://www.the-marketing-works.com/pdf/planning.pdf [retrieved 22 March 2017].

Wren, D.A. (1987) *The Evolution of Management Thought* (3rd ed.). John Wiley & Sons.

Wulf, R. (1996) 'The historical roots of Gestalt therapy theory', (pp. 1–9). http://www.gestalt.org/wulf.htm [originally appeared in the November 1996 issue of *Gestalt Dialogue: Newsletter for the Integrative Gestalt Centre*].

Yeganeh, B., and Kolb, D. (2009) 'Mindfulness and experiential learning', *OD Practitioner* 41(3): 8–14.

Zak, P.J. (2017a) 'The neuroscience of trust: Management behaviors that foster employee engagement', *Harvard Business Review* (January–February). https://hbr.org/2017/01/the-neuroscience-of-trust [retrieved 27 March 2022].

Zak, P.J. (2017b) *The Trust Factor: The Science of Creating High-performance Companies*. American Management Association.

Zaleznik, A. (1977) 'Managers and leaders: Are they different?' *Harvard Business Review* 55(May/June): 67–78.

Zes, D., and Landis, D. (2013) 'A better return on self-awareness: Companies with higher rates of return on stock also have employees with fewer personal blind spots', *Briefing 17: The Latest Thinking* (August). https://www.kornferry.com/insights/briefings-magazine/issue-17/better-return-self-awareness [retrieved 2022].

Zull, J.E. (2002) *The Art of Changing the Brain: Enriching Teaching by Exploring the Biology of Learning*. Stylus Publishing.

APPENDIX A

Summary of the RSVP Model

Relationship Mastery (People)

Primary Skills: Interpersonal Skills – collaborating, relating, developing others.

> Relationship Mastery builds followership through stakeholder engagement. Human interaction is an 'in the moment, here and now' process that benefits from a high level of emotional intelligence. Leaders attend to self and interactions with others within the immediate context of their work and the broader external environment. Relationship Mastery is enhanced when leaders track the flow of their sensations and feelings when communicating with others. Leaders are inhibited in Relationship Mastery when they are too much 'in their head'.
>
> The Relationship Mastery chapter explored the many configurations of people that leaders must engage

– e.g., individuals, groups, organizations – and some of the many auxiliary roles they must assume – e.g., mentor, coach, ally, partner, networker. Building trust, creating psychological safety, facilitating dialogue, listening actively and managing boundaries are identified as conditions conducive to fostering productive relationships.

Presence in Relationship Mastery

- *Experiencing* is the Role of Presence in Relationship Mastery.
- *In Love* is the State of Be-ing.

Strategy Mastery (Priorities)

Primary Skills. Analytical Skills – organizing, planning, managing technology.

Strategy Mastery establishes the current priorities that communicate to the company that "we are working on this and not that". It requires the ability of leaders and members of the organization to assimilate and organize ideas, strategize and plan. Intense emotions and sensations can be distractions as well as 'over-thinking' inputs. Leaders must be able to generalize and make meaning of multiple inputs and represent them in a fair and judicious manner. The process is enhanced by theoretical model building and outlining scenarios for action.

The Strategy Mastery chapter explored the ability of leaders to realize the vision by clarifying enterprise-wide priorities, allocating resources and defining processes for achieving those priorities. We recounted the storied history of "the rise and fall and rise again of strategy" followed by general guidelines for preparing an effective strategic plan that enable companies to make the adaptive shifts required in an ever-changing environment.

Presence in Strategy Mastery

- *Meaning-making* is the Role of Presence in Strategy Mastery.
- *In Justice* is the State of Be-ing.

Vision Mastery (Purpose)

Primary Skills. Information Skills – creating, gathering information, analyzing information.

>Vision Mastery offers overarching purpose and intent. It involves the ability to hold multiple realities, recognize patterns and themes, honor diversity and manage differences. Space and time are needed for reflection and creative processes to take place. Vision Mastery can be ineffective with too much brainstorming or when those participating surrender to the pressure to take action. Stillness, quietness and deep breathing help everyone stay focused. Meditation, yoga and journaling are beneficial practices that allow imagination to flow. A high level of empathy and appreciation is important.

>In the Vision Mastery chapter, we discussed the importance of leaders clarifying their aspirations for the company. We made the case for involving the

perspectives of all stakeholders in the visioning process. General guidelines for preparing a vision statement were offered, with advice to leaders to slow down and be available for reflection, even allowing themselves to 'dream' about the future state. We clarified the distinction and relationship between vision, purpose and mission that are generally included in creating a vision.

Presence in Vision Mastery

- *Noticing* is the Role of Presence in Vision Mastery.
- *In Wisdom* is the State of Be-ing.

Performance Mastery (Impact)

Primary Skills. Action – setting standards, taking action, innovating.

Performance Mastery relates to delivering on the promise to stakeholders. Leaders must confront the reality of the company's survival and success. Fostering an entrepreneurial mindset sets the stage for innovation and establishing a competitive advantage. This mastery area involves guiding and motivating others to get things done. Taking action can be inhibited by too much internal processing and an abundance of fear of risk taking. Action can be enhanced with courage, initiative taking and through instituting cycles of feedback to monitor performance.

In this chapter, we discussed Performance Mastery as the watershed position on the RSVP Model where it joins Relationship Mastery, Vision Mastery and

Strategy Mastery to complete the cycle of *what* leaders do. We expanded the scope of return on investment (ROI)[1] beyond shareholders to include all stakeholders. While we distinguished performance for leaders from employee, operational and financial performance, we maintained that leaders must have knowledge of and exercise appropriate oversight at these three levels. To help leaders respond to the complex character of performance, we recommended Ten Leadership Mindsets of Performance for Ensuring Enduring Performance.

Presence in Performance Mastery

- *Influencing* is the Role of Presence in Vision Mastery.

- *In Courage* is the State of Be-ing

---

[1] Return on investment is a mathematical formula that allows investors to compare the performance of a particular investment to those of other investments.

APPENDIX B

The Skills of *What* Leaders Do

Relationship Mastery: Interpersonal Skill Set

Eleven o'clock – ***Collaborating***

    11:00   Building a leadership team
    11:20   Building community
    11:40   Promoting partnerships and alliances

Twelve o'clock – ***Relating***

    12:00   Interacting with awareness of self, others and the environment
    12:20   Building trusting relationships
    12:40   Communicating effectively

One o'clock – ***Developing Others***

    1:00   Mentoring, inspiring and motivating others
    1:20   Giving and receiving feedback
    1:40   Empathizing

Items in the Relationship Mastery Skill Set primarily address *interpersonal abilities.* These are the abilities that enable leaders to engage with *people* effectively.

APPENDIX B (CONT'D)

The Skills of *What* Leaders Do

Vision Mastery: Information Skill Set

Two o'clock – *Creating*

    2:00   Imagining the ideal future
    2:20   Managing multiple realities, dilemmas and differences
    2:40   Exercising patience

Three o'clock – *Gathering Information*

    3:00   Clarifying purpose, mission and vision
    3:20   Assessing company climate and culture
    3:40   Monitoring the external environment

Four o'clock – *Analyzing Information*

    4:00   Recognizing industry trends and patterns
    4:20   Understanding implications of the changing environment
    4:40   Synthesizing data into practical information and reports

Items in the Vision Mastery Skill Set primarily address *information abilities* of imagining, perceiving, collecting and analyzing information. They are the abilities that enable leaders to understand our environment as they clarify *purpose*, *mission*, and *vision*.

APPENDIX B (CONT'D)

The Skills of *What* Leaders Do

Strategy Mastery: Analytical Skill Set

*Five o'clock – **Organizing***

        5:00   Applying theories for data analysis
        5:20   Utilizing statistical tools and models
        5:40   Designing operational scenarios and simulations

*Six o'clock – **Planning***

        6:00   Forecasting the future
        6:20   Creating a vision-based strategy
        6:40   Aligning goals to strategy

*Seven o'clock – **Managing Technology***

        7:00   Utilizing current technology
        7:20   Managing privacy and cyber-security risks
        7:40   Ensuring accounting controls and financial resiliency

Items in the Strategy Mastery Skill Set primarily address *analytical abilities*. These are the abilities that enable leaders to use information and technology as they *prioritize* work and the financial stability of the company.

APPENDIX B (CONT'D)

The Skills of *What* Leaders Do

Performance Mastery: Action Skill Set

Eight o'clock – ***Setting Standards***

    8:00   Committing to a diverse, equitable and inclusive workforce
    8:20   Designing systems to ensure employee well-being
    8:40   Clarifying performance goals and metrics

Nine o'clock – ***Taking Action***

    9:00   Influencing and guiding others
    9:20   Getting things done
    9:40   Being decisive

Ten o'clock – ***Innovating***

    10:00   Being a catalyst of change
    10:20   Being entrepreneurial
    10:40   Taking risks

Items in the Performance Mastery Skill Set primarily address operational or *action abilities*. These are the abilities that enable leaders to produce *outcomes* by implementing ideas, decisions, plans and solutions.

APPENDIX C

The Skills of *How* Leaders Do Their Work

Presence Mastery: Four Roles Skill Sets

Eleven, Twelve, One o'clock – *Experiencing*

Awareness of one's personal experience and awareness of others and the broader environment.

11:00	Focusing on the present moment
12:00	Attending to personal feelings
1:00	Sensing

Two, Three, Four o'clock – *Noticing*

Recognizing patterns and themes and considering experience from multiple perspectives.

2:00	Exercising patience
3:00	Observing
4:00	Considering all perspectives

Five, Six, Seven o'clock – *Meaning-making*

Using frameworks, principles, theories, generalizations and metaphors to understand experience.

5:00	Using logic and reason
6:00	Organizing ideas
7:00	Analyzing

Eight, Nine, Ten o'clock – *Influencing*

Aiming to make a difference by applying knowledge and understanding to guide future operations.

    8:00   Guiding others
    9:00   Encouraging others
   10:00   Experimenting

Items in the Four Roles of Presence Skill Sets primarily support leaders in their use-of-self as they build *relationships*, create *vision*, structure *strategy* and guide *performance*.

APPENDIX C (CONT'D)

The Skills of *How* Leaders Do Their Work

Presence Mastery: Four States of Be-ing Skill Sets

Eleven, Twelve, One o'clock – *In Love*

Willingness to extend an open heart to self and to those being led.

11:00	Acceptance and care of self
12:00	Acceptance and concern for others
1:00	Shares feelings

Two, Three, Four o'clock – *In Wisdom*

Gaining enlightenment and insight from self, from others and from additional sources of input, past and present.

2:00	Seeks discernment
3:00	Sees the whole
4:00	Appreciates silence

Five, Six, Seven o'clock – *In Justice*

Applying principles of fairness, equity and respect for all peoples.

5:00	Exercises reason
6:00	Fair minded
7:00	Advocates equality

Eight, Nine, Ten o'clock – *In Courage*

Taking risks and moving ahead with confidence and resolve despite the uncertainties involved.

8:00	Confident
9:00	Brave
10:00	Leads the way

Items in the Four States of Be-ing Skill Sets primarily focus on the *character* of the leader and support them bringing integrity and humanity to their work.

INDEX

#MeToo 23
Active listening 79, 82–3
Adaptability 139
Adaptive change 31, 33, 55, 196
Age of Not Knowing (ANK), The xvi, 2, 12, 67, 108, 129, 132, 161, 163, 171, 191
Alignment 51, 88, 111, 126, 193–5
Analyzing information 108, 112, 114, 215, 219
Antitheses 101
Aristotle 41, 193
Art of War, The 41, 119
Authoritarian leadership 42–4
Authority, Presence, Impact (API) Model, The 173
Awareness 62–4, 81, 89, 90, 113, 170–3, 177, 180, 183, 184, 193, 196
Batliwala, Srilatha 46–7
Be-ing in courage 8, 13, 166, 180, 181, 186, 187, 217, 225
Be-ing in justice 8, 13, 166, 180, 181, 184–5, 187, 215, 224

Be-ing in love 8, 13, 166, 180, 184, 187, 214, 224
Be-ing in wisdom 8, 13, 166, 180, 181, 185, 187, 216, 224
Beginning, Middle, End 63–4, 150
Being and doing 175, 176
Berra, Yogi 95, 96
Block, Peter 6, 78, 102
Boundary management 83, 85, 94, 194
Boyatzis, Richard viii, xvi, 9, 192
Business-level strategy 125–6
Calibrating presence 165, 177, 186
Carter, John v, viii, ix, xv, 177, 184
Case Western Reserve University xv, 130
Change 1–2, 10, 20, 21, 26–39, 53, 55, 57, 103–4, 113, 131, 136, 139, 145, 148–50, 160, 162, 170, 178–9, 196
Chidiac, Marie-Anne 62
Chipman, Donald 71, 73

INDEX

Climate change 19, 22, 25, 197
Clock positions 67–8, 86–94, 108–14, 129–36, 155–62, 218–25
Coel, Michaela 95–6
Collaborating 6, 21, 37, 53, 67, 86, 87–8, 93, 131, 146, 182, 195, 213, 218
Collective leadership 41, 45–6
Company-level strategy 125
Context 17–25, 26, 44, 70, 111, 113, 123, 170, 172, 191, 198
Continuous improvement 34, 146–7, 153, 185, 198
COVID-19 pandemic 20, 23, 27, 28, 99, 132, 154, 161
Creating 108, 114, 182, 215, 219
Cultivating the Four Roles of Presence 182–4
Cultivating the Four States-of-Be-ing of Presence 182, 184–6
Customers 19, 21–2, 32, 76, 78, 91, 101, 114, 119, 124, 135, 141, 145, 157, 161, 197
Delivering results 143, 149, 159
Democratic leadership 42, 43
Developing others 67, 86, 87, 91, 93, 182, 213, 218
Dialogue 70, 79, 80–2, 88, 94, 214
Dilemmas 48–50, 101, 108, 109, 134, 144, 170, 219
Dilemmas of leadership 48–50
Diversity, equity, inclusion (DEI) xvi, 23, 25, 86, 114, 148, 160, 170, 171, 178, 179, 198

Elizabeth I, Queen 119
Emergence 62, 128, 193, 196
Emergent change 31, 32, 113, 137, 196
Emotional intelligence (EQ) 73–4, 213
Ensuring enduring performance 140, 151–4, 163, 217
Evocative presence 175–6, 186
Evolution of leadership thought 41–2
Experiencing 7, 60–1, 165, 173, 180, 182, 183, 184, 186, 187, 214, 222
Experiential learning viii, xvi, 3–5, 12, 58–9, 64, 180, 182, 191
Exponential change 33, 35–6
Feedback, Giving and receiving 88, 91, 183
Feminist leadership 46–7
Finances 103, 124, 135, 143
Fixing-up the foul-ups 151–3, 163
Follett, Mary Parker 5, 41, 46, 58
Four Roles of Presence, The 7, 13, 165, 180, 182–3, 187, 223
Four States of Be-ing of Presence, The 8, 13, 166, 180–2, 184, 187, 224–5
Four types of change 33–6
Freud, Sigmund 5, 41
Functional-level strategy 126
Future Presence (Impact) 174–5

INDEX

Gathering Information 108, 110, 114, 182, 215, 219
Gaye, Marvin 17–18
General systems theory (GST) 36, 38
Generativity 193, 195–6
Gestalt Cycle of Experience 62–3
Gestalt Institute of Cleveland, The ix, xv, 5, 180
Gestalt resistances 29, 64
Gestalt theory and practice 3, 4–5, 12, 58, 61–4, 167, 191
Goleman, Daniel 73
Good listening 83, 84
Group Psychology and the Analysis of the Ego 41
Hawkins, Peter 173
Hawthorne studies 42, 71–3
Heifetz, Ronald 5, 33, 55
Hirsch, Leonard xv
Hoffer, Eric 55
Holism 5, 61, 193–4
How leaders do their work 7, 12, 68, 140, 222–5
Human Relations movement 73
iGOLD Center, The x, 27
Immigration 22–3, 25
Incremental change 33, 34, 35
Industrial Revolution 41
Influencing 8, 13, 156, 158, 166, 180–3, 186, 217, 221, 223
Innovating 28–30, 109, 124, 143, 150, 153, 156, 160–3, 182, 196–8, 216, 221

Innovation and learning capacity 124
Innovative Leader, The 198
Inquiry 32, 57, 85, 106, 127, 129, 154, 193, 195
Integrative 194
Internal processes 124, 216
International Gestalt Organization and Leadership Development Program, The – see *iGOLD Center, The*
Jones, Brenda B. viii, 2, 74
Korn Ferry Institute 73
Kotter, John 45, 98
Laissez-faire leadership 42, 43
Landis, Dana 73
Lauren, Ralph xi–xiii, 97 – also see *Ralph Lauren Corporation*
Laurie, Donald 33, 55
Leadership 2, 5–7, 19, 40–54, 55, 58, 64, 76–9, 96, 104, 121, 141, 151, 159, 166, 168, 191, 193, 199
Leadership Roles of Relating, The 76–9
Leadership Skills Profile (LSP) 94, 115, 138, 164
Learning cycle 4, 10, 59, 60
Learning modes 9, 59–60, 192
Learning styles xvii, 59, 60, 94, 115, 138, 164, 192
Learning-to-acceptance ratio in response to change 28–9
Legatum Leadership Forum, The 78, 79

INDEX

Lesbian, Gay, Bi-sexual, Transgender, Queer/Questioning, Intersex, Asexual plus (LGBTQIA+) 23
Lewin, Kurt 5, 26, 31, 42–4, 58, 61, 131
Lukensmeyer, Carolyn viii, ix, xv
Luthans, Fred 74
Managing change 27, 39
Managing or leading 45
Managing technology 126, 129, 134, 136, 182, 214, 220
Mandela, Nelson 5, 174, 181
Mary, Queen of Scots 119
McKinsey & Company 21, 56, 97, 99, 148, 157
Meaning making 8, 13, 27, 35, 39, 112, 165, 180–4, 215, 222
Miranda, Lin-Manuel 96
Mission 6, 47, 53, 96, 99–100, 107, 110–11, 114, 115, 128, 216, 219
Modes of presence 165, 175–6, 186
Montgomery, Cynthia 119, 120
Motown 18
Multiple payoff interventions 143, 147, 160
Multiple realities 6, 29, 39, 64, 101, 109, 157, 183, 185, 215, 219
National Academy of Science 72
Nevis, Edwin viii, ix, xv, 62, 167, 168
New Britain, Connecticut 44
Newman, Martyn 74
Noticing 8, 13, 61, 62, 113, 180, 181–3, 185, 216, 222
NTL Institute of Applied Behavioral Science viii, 44, 73, 83, 193
Organization & Systems Development (OSD) Program, The xv, 5, 177
Organizing 53, 68, 120, 126, 129, 130, 136, 182, 214, 220
Paradoxes 101, 150, 152
Paradoxical change 30, 39, 178
Past Presence (Authority) 174
Past, present, future 173, 186
Perceived Weirdness Index (PWI), The 165, 177, 179, 186
PWI sweet spot 179
Peres, Shimon 56
Performance Inquiry 154–5
Performance Mastery 7, 12, 68, 96, 139–64, 180–2, 192, 199, 216–17, 221
Performance Mastery Usage Indicator 162, 163
Perlman, Helen Harris 69, 70
Perspectives on change 31, 39
Peterson, Suzanne 74
Planned change 31–3, 63
Planning 32, 118, 120–4, 126–30, 132, 136, 137, 182
Politics 1, 47, 52, 172, 197
Power 22–3, 42–3, 46–7, 51, 71, 160, 165, 168, 171
Powerful questions 82–3, 90

INDEX

Powerful statements   82–3, 90
Presence Mastery   7–8, 12, 140, 165–87, 199, 222, 224
Presence Mastery in Action   180
Present Presence (Presence)   174
Principles of Presence   170
Principles of Scientific Management   41, 72
Provocative presence   175–6
Psychological safety   70, 79–80, 88, 94, 214
Purpose   1, 6, 26, 31, 47, 96, 99–100, 106, 110–11, 114, 115, 126, 128, 195, 215–16
PWI sweet spot – see *Perceived Weirdness Index*
Ralph Lauren Corporation   xi–xiii, 112 – see also *Lauren, Ralph*
Reflection   8, 49, 60, 85, 96, 101, 105–6, 215–16
Relating   10, 76, 83, 86–7, 89, 93, 94, 182, 213, 218
Relating to others   71, 76
Relating to self   74–5, 94
Relationship Inquiry   85–6
Relationship Mastery   6, 8, 12, 67, 69–94, 180, 182, 184, 213–14, 218
Relationship Mastery Usage Indicator   92, 93
Resistance   x, 29, 39, 56, 64, 111, 143, 148–9, 160, 162, 178
Resistance to learning   56–8

RSVP Fundamentals of Leadership Model, The   6–12, 36, 51, 64, 68, 71, 105, 139, 140, 141, 152, 163, 166, 191–2, 199, 213–17
Seashore, Charlie   172, 173
Self-awareness   60, 73–5, 89, 168, 171
Servant leadership   vii, 46
Setting standards   68, 155, 156, 162, 182, 216, 221
Shared leadership   45–6
Shaw, George Bernard   97
Shepard, Herb   v, ix, xvi, 179
Siminovitch, Dorothy E.   x, 62
Skills of Performance Mastery, The   155–64, 221
Skills of Relationship Mastery, The   86–94, 218
Skills of Strategy Mastery, The   129–38, 220
Skills of Vision Mastery, The   107–16, 219
Smuts, Jan   5, 193–4
Social configurations of relating, The   76
Stanford University   73
Strategic planning   118, 120–5, 128, 129, 137, 215
Strategy   6, 7, 53, 117–29, 133, 137, 142, 215, 220, 223
Strategy Inquiry   127–8
Strategy Mastery   6, 12, 68, 96, 117–38, 181–2, 199, 214–15, 217, 220
Strategy Mastery Usage Indicator   136, 137

231

INDEX

Stratford, Claire   viii, ix, 180
Strengths, Weaknesses, Opportunities, Threats (SWOT) Analysis   113, 121, 128
Sustaining the positives   151, 163
Systems   22, 32, 36–8, 55, 73, 76, 97, 109, 113, 121, 143, 145–6, 151, 157, 194
Taking action   156, 158, 162, 182, 216
Tavistock Institute   73
Taylor, Frederick   5, 41, 72
Ten Mindsets of Performance, The   143–4, 163
Thompson, Mark   56
Three Levels of Performance, The   142–3
Training groups   193
Training Group (T-group)   44
Transacting or transforming   45
Transformational change   33, 34, 35
Transitional change   33, 34–5
Trends   19–20, 25, 108, 111–12, 133, 145, 161, 162, 172, 185
Trust   9, 31, 70, 79–80, 89–90, 158, 184
Tubman, Harriet   5, 119

Tzu, Sun   5, 41, 119
Underground Railroad, The   119
Unit of Work   63, 149
United Arab Emirates Vision 2021, The   97
Unplanned change   31–3
Use-of-self   7, 13, 62, 165, 167, 170, 180, 182, 186, 223
Virtual   23, 24, 28, 30, 81, 84, 133
Vision   xii, 6, 47, 51, 53, 96–116, 120, 125, 126, 127, 133, 137
Vision Inquiry   106
Vision Mastery   6, 12, 67, 95–116, 139, 140, 181, 182, 192, 199, 215–17, 219
Vision Mastery Usage Indicator   114, 115
von Bertalanffy, Ludwig   36
Western Electric Company   72
What leaders do   6–7, 8, 10, 12, 44, 67, 68, 139–40, 186, 217, 218–21
'What's Going On'   17–18
Wyley, Chantelle   viii, x
Zaleznik, Abraham   5, 53, 97
Zes, David   73
Zoom fatigue   24

www.ingramcontent.com/pod-product-compliance
Lightning Source LLC
LaVergne TN
LVHW050841080526
838202LV00009B/310